ISBN 978-1-331-50504-4
PIBN 10199153

This book is a reproduction of an important historical work. Forgotten Books uses
state-of-the-art technology to digitally reconstruct the work, preserving the original format
whilst repairing imperfections present in the aged copy. In rare cases, an imperfection in
the original, such as a blemish or missing page, may be replicated in our edition. We do,
however, repair the vast majority of imperfections successfully; any imperfections that
remain are intentionally left to preserve the state of such historical works.

For support please visit www.forgottenbooks.com

1 MONTH OF
FREE
READING

at
www.ForgottenBooks.com

By purchasing this book you are eligible for one month membership to ForgottenBooks.com, giving you unlimited access to our entire collection of over 1,000,000 titles via our web site and mobile apps.

To claim your free month visit:
www.forgottenbooks.com/free199153

English
Français
Deutsche
Italiano
Español
Português

www.forgottenbooks.com

Mythology Photography **Fiction**
Fishing Christianity **Art** Cooking
Essays Buddhism Freemasonry
Medicine **Biology** Music **Ancient**
Egypt Evolution Carpentry Physics
Dance Geology **Mathematics** Fitness
Shakespeare **Folklore** Yoga Marketing
Confidence Immortality Biographies
Poetry **Psychology** Witchcraft
Electronics Chemistry History **Law**
Accounting **Philosophy** Anthropology
Alchemy Drama Quantum Mechanics
Atheism Sexual Health **Ancient History**
Entrepreneurship Languages Sport
Paleontology Needlework Islam
Metaphysics Investment Archaeology
Parenting Statistics Criminology
Motivational

THE

PROTESTANT EXILES

OF

ZILLERTHAL;

THEIR PERSECUTIONS AND EXPATRIATION FROM THE TYROL,
ON SEPARATING FROM THE ROMISH CHURCH AND
EMBRACING THE REFORMED FAITH.

TRANSLATED

FROM THE GERMAN OF DR. RHEINWALD

OF BERLIN.

BY JOHN B. SAUNDERS

SECOND EDITION.

LONDON:

HATCHARD AND SON, PICCADILLY; NISBET AND CO.,

BERNERS STREET.

1840.

27606

TO

HER MOST GRACIOUS MAJESTY

ADELAIDE, QUEEN DOWAGER,

𝕿𝖍𝖎𝖘 𝕹𝖆𝖗𝖗𝖆𝖙𝖎𝖛𝖊

IS, BY PERMISSION,

MOST RESPECTFULLY DEDICATED BY

HER MAJESTY'S

MOST OBEDIENT AND HUMBLE SERVANT,

THE TRANSLATOR.

ADVERTISEMENT

TO

THE SECOND EDITION.

In presenting a Second Edition of this little work, the Translator wishes to offer one observation on a criticism which has been advanced respecting his use of the term *Catholic*.

It has been objected, that he has hereby made a concession to the claims of the Romanists. Thus one writer says, (and there are elsewhere similar instances)—" We have only one observation to make: the translator says in a note, quite at the commencement, that 'throughout this narrative the word Catholic must be taken as synonymous with Roman Catholic or Anti-Pro-

A

testant;' and so having been induced to call evil good, and to put sweet for bitter, he continues to compliment his Protestant readers by informing them in every page that they are heretics by conceding to Popery the term Catholic. We are resolved never to let this dangerous inconsistency pass unnoticed, and having expressed our regret that the word Romanist was not employed where Romanist was intended, we acknowledge it to be the only drawback on much gratification experienced in reading the little history."*

To this the translator considers it sufficient to reply, that for this error, whatever it be, *he* is not responsible, but the author, inasmuch as it must be granted to be a translator's principal duty faithfully to render the words of his original. It would seem, moreover, that on the Continent the term *Catholic* is used rather in a conventional than in its strict and proper sense; for which practice an adequate reason may, perhaps, be found in the

* Christian Lady's Magazine, February, 1840.

peculiar circumstances in which the Reformation was there necessarily effected; a practice also not without example in some of the best writers of our own country, though here not to be justified, as having no plea of custom or necessity.

For these and other reasons, the translator has thought it not needful to alter his translation in this respect, deeming it sufficient to have implied his own opinion in the note referred to by the reviewer, from which it will be seen that, while he has accurately preserved the author's language, he intends no concession to the claims of Romanists.

April 23, 1840.

PREFACE.

———

THE substance of the following narrative, drawn up by Dr. Rheinwald, of Berlin, was first communicated to the " Repertory for Theological Literature and Ecclesiastical Statistics,"* a periodical of which he is the editor. It was afterwards enlarged and published in a separate form, the fourth edition of which has been used for the present translation.

The subject to which it relates was, I believe, first introduced to the English public by the Rev. Thomas Hartwell Horne, who, in a sermon preached

* " Der Allgemeine Repertorium für Theologische Literatur und kirkliche Statistik." Juni, 1837.

by him before the Corporation of the City of London, on Michaelmas-day, 1837, in comparing the civil and religious privileges of our own country with those of the Continent, took occasion to advert to the then recent case of the Protestant Tyrolese; and added in an appendix, printed with the sermon, a short statement of the facts, derived chiefly from the " Archives du Christianisme."

Subsequently, more lengthened details of the event appeared in a leading journal,* and also briefer notices in some other periodicals. But the most formal and particular notice which the subject seems hitherto to have received in this country, was an article in the Quarterly Review, No. 127, for June of the present year, containing an extended analysis of Dr. Rheinwald's narrative, together with extracts, accompanied by an able and appropriate commentary. To the present writer, however, it appeared that the story of an

* The Times Newspaper.

event so important in itself, and in its probable consequences, was well worthy of an entire English translation; and could not fail, in that form, to interest many classes in this Protestant kingdom. The fact, also, that our late revered Sovereign manifested so great a sympathy for the case of these poor people, and was the first to interfere on their behalf, will doubtless contribute to the interest of the narrative in the eyes of the British nation. An account of the part sustained by his late Majesty in this transaction will be found recorded in its proper place;* yet the mention of it here will scarcely be deemed superfluous, as it is probable that a circumstance so much to the honour of King William IV. is far less known than it deserves to be.

With respect to the moral of the story, the lessons it teaches seem to be manifold. May we not hereby learn the still unchanged spirit of intolerance and persecution of the Romish Church?

* See page 73.

Some, indeed, may object to this statement, and allege, that the evidence inculpates not the Church, but only the Austrian Government. I am very far from wishing to press, without full warrant, an accusation of this kind against a communion which has assuredly no lack of such sins to answer for; still it appears scarcely possible for any one, after having read the history with impartial attention, to doubt that the persecuting acts of the secular power were instigated by the ecclesiastical —that, in fact, what the State did in this respect, arose from its connexion with the Church, and as the executor of her desires. The Austrian Government seems ever to have inclined to a lenient policy, and to give effect to its Toleration-Edicts; but there was an influence paramount to that of law and justice, and even the Imperial will, and what was that but the dominancy of the priesthood? But leaving this as a point to be settled by private judgment, all, it is presumed, will concur in admiring the calm resignation with which these people sustained themselves under their severe trials. Although for many years deprived of what was to them most dear,—the blessings of public worship and the holy sacraments,—they yet adopted no unlawful nor unauthorized measures to supply the deficiency. Under all their maltreatments, they shewed no refractory resistance to the lawful authorities, nor intruded on the sacerdotal functions, but patiently waited until it pleased God to grant them their desires; meanwhile, "they looked immediately to Himself for a supply of that grace, the external channels of which were denied to them." Yet were they not of a too soft and yielding temper, but proved by their conduct how compatible firmness is with a humble and tranquil mind. Their earnest, self-denying piety, their ardent love of truth, by which they were enabled to forsake all most dear to them for the gospel's sake, cannot but win our respect, and, one would hope, will excite in some a holy emulation. Happily, we are not required to make the like sacrifices, but all who would be truly Christ's disciples must be partakers of the same spirit.

There are also several other lessons which appear fairly deducible from the narrative before us— as the great value of religious instruction, and church ordinances, the superiority of scriptural education over every other; for these people, though unlettered according to the world's phrase, seem to have possessed, by virtue of their acquaintance with the Word of God, a clearer and more vigorous understanding, as well as a purer conscience, than many who have been most deeply taught in the learning of the schools. This is not said with a view to depreciate secular learning in its proper place, but only to urge its due subordination to that which is unquestionably the highest wisdom. But these and many other inferences of great practical moment I rather leave to the reader's reflection, than detain him with any observations of my own.

It may be well to add, that the account here

given by Dr. Rheinwald was compiled not only from the materials presented by the various journals in which, on both sides, the subject has been largely discussed on the Continent, but that it is also the result of his own personal knowledge, " for he himself visited the inhabitants in their native land, and formed his notions of their doctrine, their habits, and their conduct, from actual observation." And now the narrative is commended to the reader, with the hope that in its present form it may subserve the interests of truth and piety, and that its perusal may promote in all a juster appreciation and improvement of our own privileges, civil and religious.

THE TRANSLATOR.

December, 1839.

CONTENTS.

CHAPTER I.

CHAPTER II.

CHAPTER III.

CHAPTER IV.

CHAPTER V.

CHAPTER VI.

THE EXILES OF ZILLERTHAL.

CHAPTER I.

Situation and employments of Zillerthal—Property of the Inhabitants—Their Religion—The Saltzburg Persecution—
Schaitberger—Protestant Movements in the Tyrol—Applications for dismissal from the Romish Church—Audience
with the Emperor Francis — Catholic Reaction — Prince
John and the Archbishop in the Valley—Petition to leave
the Country—Government Edict.

Such various and, in some measure, conflicting
reports,* have for several years been circulated
respecting the religious movement in the Tyrol,
that it has become necessary to treat the matter
somewhat in detail, especially as it has now taken
a decisive direction.

* Dr. Rheinwald here recites in a long note, which it does
not appear necessary to present in full, the names of several
journals and other publications, in which the matter was fully
discussed both on the side of the Romanists and Protestants,
and thus evinces not only the great interest which the subject

But before proceeding to the subject itself, it will be useful to premise some particulars respecting the district and its local peculiarities.

In journeying from Saltzburg to Innsbruck, when the traveller has proceeded full two-thirds of the distance, not far from Rattenberg and Schwatz, on the road to the village of Strass, there opens before him, between two majestic masses of rock, a wide and lovely valley. It is watered by the clear and fertilizing Ziller, which issuing from the Southern Alps, flows into the Inn, immediately below Strass, and gives to the valley its name. The path winds along to the right of the stream, on both sides of which lie the villages of Brugg, Iming, Schlitters, Kapsing, &c.* Nearly in the middle, is the little town of Zell, the seat of a Deanery and a Landgericht,† below which the wild Gerlos unites with the Ziller. The whole

---

has excited in Germany, but also his industry in collecting materials for his own narrative. Indeed he seems not to have omitted any method by which he might make himself acquainted with all the particulars.— *Tr.*

* The villages are thus enumerated by the author: Brugg, Iming, Schlitters, Fugen, Kapsing, Uderns, Neid, März, Slum, Kaltenbach, Aschack, Rohr, Hüppach, Ramsau, Unter and Oberdichl, Hollenzen, Maierhof, Brandberg, Finkenberg.

† Landgericht, a kind of local court for the administration of justice, &c.

extent from the Inn to the Tristenspitz, which overlooks and closes in the valley, is about five miles.* As far as Zell, the valley is of a tolerably equal breadth, but below that town it becomes narrower, ascending eastward to the steep wall of the Gerlos, southward to the Schwendauer Falls, and then again on the east, losing itself towards the Dreieckspitz.† On both sides of the valley, rich meadows alternate with heavy arable land, at little distances diversified with the villages, with their pretty white houses, some with outside galleries, interspersed with farms, manors, chapels, inns, penfolds, &c.; all overlooked by the surmounting green-clad church-spires, which with their golden crosses form an appropriate ornament to the neighbourhood. On the right and left, behind the pastures, mountains arise to an immense height, some clothed with wood, and with naked summits; on others are well-cultivated meadows, parted into squares, having in the midst one or more cottages. From the commencement of the spring till the end of the Alpine season, these are the resort of herdsmen with their cattle. A refreshing wind prevails on these heights, from

* A German mile is equal to 4½ miles English.
† i.e. Triangular Peak.

which there is a charming prospect of a region luxuriant in vegetation, and animated with industrious labourers, numerous flocks, and merrily sporting inhabitants. But for travellers the evenings are generally the most attractive, when the Ave-Maria is heard resounding from the high towers,* mingled with the distant tinkling of the sheep-bells, and when at a later hour, all forms having vanished, the slopes are suddenly illumined with the lights in the scattered mountain-huts. With the exception of some small portions belonging to the Innthal, the valley is divided into two Landgerichts, (Fügen and Zell,) and contains, in fourteen pastoral stations, between 15 and 16,000 inhabitants. These gain their livelihood chiefly by agriculture and the rearing of cattle. The latter, followed here in the greater proportion and with extraordinary success, occasions many to go abroad, and not unfrequently into remote parts, as Petersburg, Cracow, Odessa, and Constantinople. The less opulent endeavour to find employment in Styria and Carinthia by felling forests, &c.; a smaller number are mechanics in the foundries and

---

* During this while, the people say their evening prayers, and in the summer season, outside of their cottages.—See the Frontispiece.

manufactories of the Lower Innthal. Yet without these foreign resources, they would be well able to find subsistence, as their meadows, herds, and forests supply their necessary wants, and of imaginary ones, especially in the upper valley, they have few or none. In general, property is pretty equally distributed; there is nowhere urgent want, and a street-beggar is scarcely ever to be seen. Compared with other valleys, (the Pintzgau for instance,) the farms, on account of the abundant population and plentifulness of money, fetch a high price. A farm of " three cows," which produces scarcely sufficient corn for the consumption of its possessor, costs 3000 florins. In the Upper and Lower Pintzgau, a farm of ten or twelve cows, with a proportionate quantity of arable land, might be purchased for the same money. The inhabitants are strong, healthy, and well formed, but less remarkable for regularity of features and beauty of countenance, than those in Dur and the Innthals. Both here and in the neighbouring valleys, there are still to be found many traces of the well-known Tyrolese manners,* much more frequently than in

* " They are a free, lively, and resolute people, that do not belie the character of the mountain folk." The authority for this is Voelter, a deacon of Wurtemberg, who visited Ziller-thal just as the Exiles were about departing.

the south, which is inhabited by a mixed race, blending both the German and Italian character.

Good-nature, frankness, and friendliness are expressed in their countenances, and in their hearty greeting of the traveller, by whom these qualities are, on a closer acquaintance, further recognised. It is true that their joviality is not unfrequently mingled with a degree of rudeness and extravagance. This is especially exhibited in their fighting and wrestling matches, in their predilection for animal combats, in their free and unrestrained dances,* and in the excessive loudness of their national songs, so peculiarly characteristic of the people. It must moreover be esteemed a fortunate circumstance for these districts, that they have hitherto remained tolerably free from the intrusion of foreigners and continental idlers, though, from the example of Saltzburg, southern Bavaria, &c., it is much to be feared that they will not wholly escape such corrupting influence.

According to their religious profession, the inhabitants of the valley belong to the Roman-catholic Church. The ecclesiastical jurisdiction

---

* When modern travellers, as Lewald and others, speak of " the convulsive, cramp-like dances," we must not consider them as including Zillerthal. They are found indeed in Dur, its near vicinity, but are by peculiar circumstances confined to that district.

is shared by the two Bishops of Brixen and Saltzburg, the Ziller forming the boundary of their respective dioceses. A large proportion of the Zillerdalers are obedient to the Church: custom has
maintained its dominion over them. They are
Catholics,* because their parents, ancestors, neighbours, the respectable people, and the Emperor
himself, are so. They also find it convenient,
and have no particular reason to desire a change.
Catholics, however, in the strict Roman sense of
that term, such as are to be found in Dur, in
southern Tyrol, and (formerly at least) in the
south-east portion of the Lower Innthal, are here
proportionably much rarer. This, indeed, is
almost confessed by the Catholic journals themselves, when they lament over the want of piety
in the Zillerthal; a complaint, the truth of which
we also concede, though in quite another sense.
In the valley, there is a very large number
wholly given over to indifferency, who outwardly
retain themselves to the Church and observe its
ceremonies, it may be from political or from family
motives, but who, when they meet with others
like-minded with themselves, do not hesitate to

* Throughout this narrative, the word Catholic must be taken
as synonymous with Roman Catholic, or Anti-Protestant.— *Tr.*

declare their real opinions. These are chiefly
itinerant tradespeople, or roving minstrels, who,
having travelled abroad by sea and land, have,
by their intercourse with others in theatres and
taverns, become " enlightened." Recently, however, there has appeared in the valley another religious party, quite distinct from those hitherto
described, which, though the smallest as to numbers, has yet, upon other grounds, the strongest
claims to our attention.

In order duly to comprehend its origin and character, it will be necessary to glance at the Ecclesiastical History of a neighbouring district, the
archbishopric of Saltzburg. Here also was the
voice heard, which, in the sixteenth century, went
forth from Wittenburg. Pious men, as John
Staupitz, Paul Speratus and others, awakened and
cherished the love of the gospel. Everywhere in
town and country the call found an echo, especially
among the miners in the south and south-western
parts of the diocese. The new doctrine was but
little aided by the superior ranks, and sharply
opposed (especially since the time of Rudolph the
Second) on the Austrian frontiers; notwithstanding, there arose many Lutheran congregations,
which were in the most flourishing condition, when,

in the year 1729, the Archbishop, Count Firmian decreed against them that persecution from which the arm of Frederic William, with the entire body of Protestants, was able to protect them no further than by obtaining for them the right of emigration. The consequence of this event was a lasting impression of terror. Neither in the reign of Joseph, when the mild Hieronymus governed in Saltzburg, nor later, during the French-Bavarian period, nor afterwards (since 1815) under Austria's new guarantees for Liberty of Conscience and Belief, do we hear any tidings of Protestant communities in Saltzburg. Most erroneously, however, should we thence conclude that they had no existence. It is true that force and stratagem had, to an incredible degree, endeavoured to search out and extirpate all those who were disaffected to the Roman Faith; yet a seed of Protestantism still remained. Especially was this the case in the Upper Pintzgau, the frontier of the present Tyrol, and in Teffereck-euthal, which now belongs to the circle of Pusterthal. From these places there went forth a constant and active influence upon the Tyrolean districts, which became conspicuous not only in the provinces of the interior, but also in the capital itself. The Lutherans in and about Innsbruck

were sought out and persecuted, as they were in
the time of the Saltzburg emigration; but many
more remained unobserved, who secretly cherished
the gospel in Zillerthal,* and the surrounding less
frequented valleys.

Their religious knowledge was here partly obtained from the visits of other inhabitants, but
partly and chiefly it was derived from books.
Among these, next to the Bible itself, the work of
Joseph Schaitberger occupies the highest place.
Schaitberger was a miner of Saltzburg, who, already, before the great persecution under Firmian,
had been imprisoned on account of his belief, and
as he steadfastly adhered to his profession, and
moreover had re-asserted it by a written statement
from his prison, he was afterwards banished the
country.   At Nürnberg, he sent forth, among other
pious writings, his "Evangelical Epistle."   In this
he comforts and encourages his fellow-believers who
remained behind, and explains to them in brief the
substance of the faith.   On account of its intelligible style, as well as being the work of a layman,

* Baron Von Moll, (as the Catholic journals relate,) whose
father was, at the close of the eighteenth century, Landrichter
at Zell, says in his letter concerning Zillerthal, "Many unite
in the exercises of religion, but have another kind at home."

it obtained extensive circulation and regard; and not only stimulated the joy of the faithful, but awakened many more, both in the author's birth-place, and also in the neighbouring districts. In Zillerthal especially, many copies were dispersed, which came to be regarded as family property, and had, as we shall see hereafter, a lasting influence. Other religious writings, not always indeed of the choicest kind, found their way into these regions; the inhabitants themselves brought back to the valley many books which they had acquired during their emigrations. These journeys, undertaken for the purposes of commerce, form another parti-cular to be noted as having influenced the move-ment among the people. The Tyrolese were always accustomed, as they are at the present day, to travel on business to Franconia, Suabia, and the Rhine. In these, for the most part, Protestant countries, they formed with the inhabitants mani-fold connexions, which, by repeated visits, became closer and more important. To any one acquainted with the manner in which such circumstances originate and are developed, it cannot but appear surprising that others should have talked of an " intention to, seduce," and of " proselytizing ten-dencies." The Tyroler, when he enters a house with his wares, is accustomed to talk freely concerning his journey, or his native country, whence a conversation arises, which perhaps is carried on much further. Others stay overnight in the houses of the mechanics and peasants, and remain with them on the Sundays and festivals. In such a peasant's house, it is customary to have prayer before and after meals, as well as in the morning and evening. On Sundays, in the morning and afternoon, they go to church; afterwards some one reads out a hymn or sermon, the Tyroler being present and uniting with the family. In the circles which belong more to the so-called Pietists, the people, on Sundays and Festivals, frequent the "Hours;" when some speak, or read passages from Arndt, Steinhofer, &c., or sing chorals. The Tyroler, if he has acquired a mind for these things, is permitted to take his part therein. Should he, on his visit the next year, come again to the same house, he meets with a friendly reception, and receives, if he so request, a small New Testament, a copy of "Hiller," or a little "treasury" for his pocket. In all this, the people treat the Tyroler as they are accustomed to do the inland wanderer; they are rejoiced when a man, who, from his childhood having been taught nothing, has been only the ever-revolving machine of priestcraft, feels himself drawn by the Word of God, and gradually awakened to a new life. It thus came to pass, that the Tyrolese returned home quite others than when they departed, bringing back with them not temporal goods merely, but such as abide for ever.

It must not, however, be concealed, that while such beneficial consequences resulted from their intercourse with Protestants, there were instances of quite an opposite character. The writer himself is acquainted with several cases, wherein Catholic Tyrolese, on coming to Protestants' houses, received, at least for the time, great spiritual injury. When the Tyroler in the morning on rising or at table, signed his cross or counted his rosary, there were not wanting men who laughed and mocked at him for so doing. With others it fared much worse. "Enlightened" peasants and mechanics who had read the Penny Magazine, shewed to the Tyroler how absurd it was to confess his sins, to believe in miracles, &c. Others went so far as to declare the "Parson's babble to be all nonsense," and to prophesy the dawning of a "new era." On the strangers this made various impressions; some coincided, others fled back to the church. A Tyroler who still remains a Catholic, answered such a one, " That you may hold here in this country, but with us it still remains just as it was." From the Protestant pulpits, also, there went forth a very unequal influence. Some of the Tyrolese relate the deep religious impressions which they received from such discourses, and which at all times since they have retained. Others of another character worked a chilling and repelling effect. So said, for example, an inhabitant of the Upper Innthal, " that he had thought with himself, that if a man speaks thus among the Protestants, where the pure Word of God ought to be, the best thing at last that can be done is, to keep away from church altogether." In this way Protestant influences had for some time been working in the Zillerthal, especially in the southern district, where, at length, in several parishes, persons simultaneously finding themselves possessed of the same sentiments, communicated one with another, and formed together a little religious community. By this mutual intercourse, their Protestant impression, both in life and doctrine, became more and more refined, and attained a firmer and more perfect form. The consequence was, that the disaffection which had long relaxed the inward bond, by which they had been attached to the church, became now also manifested in externals. It is true that some still performed their part at sermons, sacraments, processions, the veneration of the sacred elements, &c. But if these thus acted not without reluctance, there were others who decisively tore themselves away, as deeming such things, according to the Word of God, to be idolatry. In short, among all, the natural desire was excited to be able to come forward publicly with their Protestant confession, and to exchange their hitherto painfully embarrassing situation for that of a legally recognised community. Besides, with many, their experience in the Word of God had so sharpened and purified their sensibility to the truth, that such a false position became, at length, quite intolerable. Accordingly, a number of men, heads of families, resolved to take the legal step for proceeding in the matter. Bartholomew Heim, J. Ram, Francis Steinlechner, James Kreidel, and his two grown-up sons, Matthias and Joseph, Matthias Drubmaier, James and George Hanser, from the villages of Ramsberg, Hollenzen, Maierhof, and Unterdichl, applied, in the summer of 1826, to their respective priests, for the " Six weeks' instruction." According to the law of the country, every one who wishes to go over to another creed, is obliged to receive such a course from his confessor, and to take a certificate thereof to the magistrate.* By the clergy this step was not unexpected; they already knew some to have outwardly separated from the church, and of others, because they had declared it at confession, that they read the Scriptures to their edification. For the rest, who were regarded as confirmed heretics, there was, on the part of the hierarchy, nothing further to be done. To these their applications some of the ecclesiastics opposed themselves with moderation. Gottsamer, since dead, at that time Dean of Zell, behaved to them with great kindness; he entered into their objections, replying to them with mildness, and expressed the hope that the matter would be amicably terminated. In other parishes, on the contrary, both sides obstinately defended their own views, and, instead of uniting, were only driven further apart. From one of their priests the Protestants

* And then "the magistrate gives the so-called 'Meldezettel,' that is, a written permission to frequent Protestant worship. Without the priest's certificate, the magistrate cannot grant the permission, and without this written permission no one bred a Roman Catholic dare be present at Protestant worship, or be received into a Protestant community."—Quar. Rev. vol. lxiv. p. 123.

separated with the declaration that they, according to the example of Josiah, (2 Chron. xxxiv. 2,) would turn neither to the right hand nor to the left. As in the meanwhile new applications for the "Instruction" continued to come in, the clergy unanimously resolved for the present to refuse them, and to apply to Innsbruck for further directions. The government communicated the matter to the two ordinaries, who approved of the measures adopted by the chapter of Zell, and protested against any establishment of a Protestant worship in the country. Thereupon the government at Innsbruck referred the matter to the Imperial Court. Five years elapsed without any decision; during which period the number of applicants for the instruction had increased more than tenfold. Already, in the beginning of the year 1832, there might have been named two hundred and forty individuals inclined to Protestantism, being, for the most part, shepherds, mechanics, labourers, &c.; a few of them farmers and freeholders. In the summer of that year, the Emperor Francis visited the Tyrol. The Protestants sent from their midst a deputation of three men, John Fleidl, Bartholomew Heim, and Christian Brucker, to Innsbruck. There the Imperial Councillor Sondermann, to whom their cause was referred by the local government, sent them an advocate, who drew up a petition, in which they expressed their decided wish to erect a filial congregation, which, at certain times in the year, should be visited by a Protestant pastor.

The Emperor received them with his usual courtesy, read their petition, and then questioned them in the following manner :—" Well, who, then, disturbs you in your belief ?" — *The Deputies.* " The Clergy."—*Emp.* " What, then, do you believe ?"—*Dep.* " We believe the words of Holy Scripture, according to the principles of the Augsburg Confession."—*Emp.* " You believe in Christ, even as I, do you not ? But in Italy there are people who do not believe in Christ at all ; that grieves me."—*Dep.* " Yes, we believe in Christ as our Lord and Saviour, and only Redeemer ; but they will not suffer us in the Zillerthal to say this."—*Emp.* " It is not permitted for the Catholics to oppress and insult you, any more than for you to insult them. Formerly, over there in Saltzburg, the Lutherans were not tolerated ; but it is now no longer so ; I oppress no one on account of his belief. But how, then, did you come by your present opinions ?"—*One of the Deputies.* " We have had the Holy Scriptures among us longer than we can ascertain. We have Bibles which are more than two hundred years old. My grandfather was aged ninety-eight years, and died only three years ago, and he had read the Scriptures from his childhood, and so has my father, and so have I, and many others; the doctrine was instilled by their parents."—*Emp.* " Indeed; there is perhaps a remnant of the Saltzburgers remaining: were you Saltzburgers ?"—*Dep.* " Yes, we belonged to the Saltzburg territory sixteen years ago."—*Emp.* " So, then, you are not willing to remain in the Catholic Church."—*Dep.* " Our conscience does not permit us; we should otherwise be hypocrites." —*Emp.* " No, that I do not wish ; I will see what can be done for you." As the people, on depart-ing, again urged their request, and assured the Emperor " that they were brave people, who had suffered no punishment, and begged that he would not forget them, nor believe anything which might be said against them; he replied, " I will not forget you, nor believe anything bad of you." The news of this interview excited great attention in the Valley. Their protestations were declared to be " lies;" yet it was deemed advisable that some counter-steps should be taken. Several congrega-tions of the Landgericht of Zell likewise sent a deputation to the Emperor, who deprecated any religious divisions in the country, and prayed, lest the bond of the nationality should thereby be loosened, that the petition of the Protestants might not be granted. The matter was soon after discussed at the Tyrolese Diet, at which several in the rank of burghers and farmers shewed a disposition towards toleration. Dr. Maurer, the burgomaster, a distinguished and esteemed inhabitant of the capital, urgently expressed his opinion that the people should be allowed to live according to their own belief. In the meanwhile, the clergy and nobility sent a petition to the local government, in which it was asserted that the Toleration Edict had never been published in these districts, and could not now have an *ex post facto* application.* Towards the middle of the year 1834, the Protestants received from Vienna the following

* " A pretence which could deceive no one acquainted with the facts of the case. When the Emperor Joseph published his edicts, he sent them to the sovereign prelates, the Prince Archbishop of Saltzburg and the Bishop of Brixen. It is true that they quietly deposited them in the archievs ; but that does not at all alter the state of the case. The fact that the Emperor sent them to these two prelates for publication and execution is quite sufficient to shew that his Imperial will was that they should serve as law in their respective dioceses ; and more is not needful to prove that the Zillerdalians were entitled to the full enjoyment of all the liberty which they conferred."—Quat. Rev. vol. lxiv. p. 127.

decision, dated April 2 :—" We find it impossible to accede to your request. If, however, you are desirous to leave the Catholic Church, you are at liberty to settle in another province of the empire, where there are already Protestant congregations." To such a transportation, however, the greater number shewed no disposition. They had already directed their eyes to a foreign country, and accordingly, in the summer of this year, some of them requested a passport. The next spring they received the following answer :—

" It is hereby notified to those persons who on the 30th of August of the last year applied for a passport to go into foreign parts, that in pursuance of the official intimation of the 15th, received in the present month, that application, according to the high Government decree of Feb. 6, must be refused, on the ground that the granting of a passport for the purpose of their future emigration is neither necessary nor allowable, inasmuch as, conformably to the Imperial Resolution of April 2, 1834, if they cannot alter their religious views, and so cannot, or will not, remain in the Tyrol, they have only to transport themselves over into another Austrian province, where there are already Protestants ; on the other hand, by a statement of good conduct and property qualification, even their foreign reception for the purpose of a formal emigration can be effected without cost, through the authorities, and then a personal appearance for buying into the foreign country will be necessary."

" Given at the Imperial Landgericht of Zell on the Ziller, March 7, 1835.   (Signed)   " SCHLECHTER."

" To the applicants
B. Heim and J. Fankhauser."

Not long after this, the Archduke John, the brother of the deceased Emperor, visited the Tyrol. The Zillerdalers were requested by their Land-gericht to seek an audience with him; whereupon three of them appeared before the Prince. They told him how often they had requested a passport; that they were as sheep without a shepherd, and yet that the deceased Emperor had promised them every good. In reply, it was intimated to them that they had misunderstood the Emperor; that he had promised them toleration, not in the Tyrol, but only generally in the Imperial States.—*The Deputies.* " No, we well understood him, because he spoke to us so distinctly. We prayed him to grant us toleration in our own family circles." As they now were warned to make no further stir about the matter, and to take care lest, in the end, it should cost some of them their heads, they repeated their wish to see personally their Emperor Ferdinand. *The Archduke.* "To orderly subjects it is permitted to go to the Emperor. Give in your request at the bailiwick; you will not be refused a passport to Vienna."—*Dep.* " Ah! if we could do that, then we should have hope. The late Emperor Francis was a good emperor and a brave man; and after a good father, as the proverb says, there comes a good son." As there were present at this audience several nobles of the province, and among them the Captain of the Circle* from Schwatz, one of the Deputies thought this a fair opportunity to demonstrate their moral conduct and good deportment as citizens. " Indeed," said he to the Prince, " I think we are orderly subjects; my lord the Captain cast all kinds of bad accusations against me when I went to Schwatz; but to-day the superintendent of our parish is in Zell, whom I can fetch, and here is the Landgericht, and there are also three witnesses present; if now any one knows anything wrong of me, though it be only a little point, I will suffer double punishment, and so also will the others; nothing shall be concealed." On this declaration, there followed no accusation from the other side.

In the summer of 1836, the Archbishop of Saltzburg, Prince Schwartzenberg, came into the valley. He ordered several of those inclined to Protestantism to be brought before him, and represented to them that they ought to remain in the church. His mild demeanour inspired them with confidence; they laid before him the authors according to which they thought themselves bound to belong to

* *Kreishauptmann;* an officer whose powers resemble those of our county lords lieutenant.

the Protestant communion, and begged that they might be permitted to attach themselves to that church. Whereupon he observed, " That would be as if you wished to throw yourselves into the fire; to that I cannot consent."

Relying on the fore-named promises, they re-newed their applications for a passport to Vienna. Meanwhile, these were disregarded; the only reply to them was a repetition of what had been said before, " that it would be a great affront to the Emperor if they were again so to trouble him." Hereupon, in the course of the year 1836, these people formed the resolution, which also they communicated to the authorities, to forsake the Valley, and to seek an asylum in foreign parts. In January, 1837, a resolution was taken in Vienna, which in the month of March was published by the Captain of the Circle in the various districts, by which, as they preferred foreign emigration, they were directed to leave the country. A term of four months from the date of publication was granted for settling their affairs. For the further-ance of their purposes in a foreign land, one of their leaders obtained, on application, the following official certificate :—

" According to the express will of his Majesty the Emperor, those inhabitants of the Zillerthal who have declared their intention of forsaking the Catholic Church are desired to leave the Tyrol, and either to emigrate into a foreign land, or to find a domicile in another Austrian province, where there are communities of the same religious creed that they themselves profess. John Fleidl, and those his companions who have declared their preference for an entire emigration, are hereby authorized to take such measures for the finding a convenient place of settlement as may be necessary in consequence of the official order of the 8th instant.

" From the Imperial Landgericht of Zell on the Ziller,
" 11th of May, 1837.

(Signed) " SCHLECHTER."

CHAPTER II.

Internal circumstances of the Protestants—Form of their Ecclesiastical life—Treatment of the Protestant Children in
the Catholic Schools—Behaviour of the Priests to the sick
and dying—Religious conversation in the year 1832—Conferences of the Clergy with several Dissidents—Controversial Sermons—Refusal of the marriage-tie, passports,
&c.—Manner of the funerals—Extra-ecclesiastical assemblies—Adherence to the Bible among the Protestants—
Their freedom from extravagances and sectarianism—Their
leaders Heim and Fleidl—Heim's house a central point of
union—The books in possession of the Protestants—Their
want of School instruction and of the Holy Eucharist.

BEFORE we further pursue the course of events,
let us contemplate more closely the circumstances
in which these people were placed by those which
have been already narrated.   If their former situation was a painful one, it was now, since the refusal of the six-weeks' instruction, doubly unsettled

and embarrassing. They saw themselves, indeed, in an unhappy dilemma. Devoted in heart to the Protestant church, they yet could not, and dared not, turn to it, though they willingly would have contributed to a church and school-system all needful support. From the Catholic church inwardly separated, they yet formally belonged to it, as not having received their dismissal, and because their civil relationships were manifoldly implicated with the ecclesiastical. It thus occurred that their religious life assumed the following forms: (1.) The new-born children of those inclined to Protestantism were brought into the Catholic churches and there baptized; the parents not being present, and the sponsors belonging to the church. (2.) The grown-up children, so soon as they had attained the age prescribed by law, were constrained, as having been baptized in the church, to attend the local schools. They were likewise required to partake of the Holy Communion, which, in these countries, is administered to children at the age of eight or nine years. (3.) The Catholic rite of marriage was refused to those disposed to Protestantism. (4.) Both in sermons and the confessional, the Catholics were warned against all intercourse with them, and the poor were forbidden to ask any alms or shelter from the "Evangelicals;"* neither were domestics and labourers to receive from them any service or employment. (5.) The priests came to the sick, admonishing them to recant and to be reconciled to the church, promising them, on this condition, the Holy Viaticum. (6.) Those who died holding sentiments opposed to the church were not received into the Catholic burial-ground.

It is evident from what has been hitherto described, that the clergy had not overstepped their authority, and even if they did somewhat encroach, their instructions and discipline were designed as well to preserve their own flocks from the infection, as to arrest those who had gone astray. But when, as a reason for the first and second of the above-mentioned procedures, it is further alleged that the parents were deluded—that the poor children ought not to suffer on that account by having the sacramental blessing withheld from them—that rather, since they had properly no

---

* Two poor Protestants had their habitation under the roof of a Catholic peasant. When the priest at M—— discovered this, he desired the peasant no longer to give them shelter. They, in consequence, would have been destitute of any home, had not the Protestant J. K., though in needy circumstances, taken them under his roof."—*Appelius.*

parents of their own, the obligation was greater to
provide for their salvation by means of Christian
sponsors and school instruction,—we must then
not only deny the proposition to be strictly appli-
cable, but must also inquire how such a tender
care for the children of Protestants, introduced
and retained by the clergy in Catholic schools, was
realized in practice. Since the period of this separation of the Protestants, the clergy had deemed
it necessary to keep a stricter watch over the education of the people, and even to put a hand
thereto in respect of their religious instruction.*

* This demonstration on the part of the Protestants appears
also, in other respects, to have worked a beneficial influence on
the Catholic Church, and especially by enlivening the zeal of
the clergy. At least, the Catholic journals report, "That in
consequence of the increase in the population dwelling at great
distances on the steep mountains, the number of helping priests
was increased, and more filial schools were erected. The assailed doctrines became, of necessity, more the subjects of discussion and proof in sermons and discourses than heretofore.
On the mountains, the so-called house-lectures were more frequently held in spacious rooms, or, in fine weather, in the open
air, followed by certain prayers on the Sundays and festivals.
It thereby happened, that among the inhabitants of the valleys
the Catholic religion received a new impulse, which was especially exhibited by the rising youth, who became in all respects
much improved, more modest, and better conducted. They
now no longer resorted so frequently to the dances; and even
the national costume of the other sex, so little corresponding to

Some schoolmasters who, with a well-meant intention, had kept back their instructions on the points
of difference, were, for so doing, degraded and dis-
placed, while that method of teaching was brought
forward in the most marked and prominent manner. Not only were the adverse doctrines condemned, but their adherents were anathematized,
and so individually and minutely described, that
the children could not fail to perceive that a
father, brother, or neighbour, was intended. The
Protestant children now became confused; their
schoolfellows laughed at them; and on going home
there were many disputes and provocations. The
children, in consequence, would not any longer go
to the school, and this was imputed to their parents,

female delicacy, began to be changed essentially for the better.
The service of God was more diligently attended, the holy Sacrament received with greater zeal, and good books of prayer
and edification were diffused among the people. Where, for
example, in former years, two priests went on Sundays to the
confessional at five o'clock in the morning, and had finished by
seven or half-past seven, there are now generally three who
give themselves to the work at the hour of four, and at the later
service are occupied with it until nine or ten. The last Jubilee
appointed by Gregory XVI. was observed with great zeal, and
the many general confessions afforded no uncertain signs of a
moral reformation. And, in general, the instructions in the
churches have been more edifying, since the separatists have
ceased to visit them."

and alleged as proof of their ungovernable obstinacy and rudeness. Children of other parents, as, for instance, those of Farmer Heim, did not wish to neglect their school, but went again by the direction of their father, and gave such excellent answers to their teacher, and proposed to the latter such questions in return, as were no less astonishing to the other children than embarrassing to the master. Scholars of such sort were expelled the schools, "because they were pert and unmannerly, resembled their parents, wished to be cleverer than their priests, did not come to the communion," &c. In other schools, different means were resorted to in order to get rid of the children. "But I shall still send both mine to the school," said a mother to the author, full of noble scorn; "yet a month ago George came home and said, 'Now the schoolmaster has made two tables; at one he places the Christian children, at the other the devil's children; at this we sit, I and Mary and Hanser's three.' "*

Not less extraordinary, and as little befitting the

---

* Another instance is given in the "Auserlesene Erzählungen." "The clergy said to the children, ' You will neither go to heaven, nor to the churchyard.' The children, ' We are content if we go to the same place as our parents.'"

dignity of their office, as well as contrary to their
" Instruction,"* was the conduct of the clergy to
the sick among the Protestants. At the commencement of their visits, they commonly made
gentler or stronger reproaches concerning their
apostasy. If the sick man answered nothing, he
was offered reconciliation with the church by
means of the Sacrament. But if he expressed any
objections, he was immediately assured by the
ecclesiastic, that in case of his refusal he could be
granted no place in God's acre,† no prayers, no
masses for his soul. Still worse it fared with
others. Long had a priest wearied himself with a
countryman named Simon Hanser. When he saw
him approaching his end, he called out to him,
" Hanser, thou art going straight to the devil." A
wood-cutter was struck down by the fall of a tree ;
his wound was thought incurable. While he was

* According to this, the priest is obliged, even though not
called in, to visit the sick man once. Should he omit, the
local authorities are to make a representation thereof. But it is
expressly said that " the priest shall proceed with all possible
moderation, kindness, and Christian love, forbear from all com-
pulsion ; and if the sick person will not receive his assistance,
then to withdraw without any further ado."

† " Gottesacker," an expressive term for a consecrated
burial-ground.

in a state of insensibility, he received the Host from a priest who was called in by the others. When he recovered, he shewed great surprise at the circumstance, and retained his connexion, as formerly, with his Protestant brethren.

Can one now wonder if there also occurred scenes of another kind which bordered on fanaticism? A shepherd on his death-bed fell into great mental anguish, and longed most earnestly to receive the Holy Eucharist. As none of those who had hitherto been his religious associates ventured to administer the Sacrament, he at last resolved to request it at the hand of the priest; to his wife, however, this appeared as nothing less than a decisive recantation, and she accordingly used every effort to prevent it. When all would not avail, she lay down on the bed by her husband's side, and with her hand presented to his mouth what appeared to him to be offered by the priest.

But we must now pass on to another important point, to examine how the Catholic clergy behaved towards the Protestants, in respect of their teaching and instruction, as to their Catholic errors. In the summer of 1832, a religious conference took place at Unterdichl, in the house of Joseph Hanser. The dissidents assembled in great numbers: among the clergy who were present was P. Sander, Dean of Zell. Before the colloquy began, one of the priests asked John Fleidl, how it came to pass that the Jews were averse to know anything about the New Testament. *Fleidl.* " Rather this asto-nishes me, that many Christians who have the Scripture, and say they believe in it, do neverthe-less not read therein. We cannot take it so much amiss in the Jews, because they, through money, were once deceived by the watchers at the grave."

The Protestants now desired that the Bible might be made the ground of the discussion. This was conceded ; but the matter soon became again perplexed, in consequence of the clergy introduc-ing such points as, the number of the Sacraments, Indulgences, the Sacred Elements, and making them the chief subjects of discourse.

When on the doctrine of the Sacraments, the conversation turned on the Unction, and the pas-sage in St. James, chap. v., being alleged for it, one of the priests read out the 14th verse. He then asked some of those present, whether they did not apprehend that, seeing that it was com-manded by the holy Apostle with the clearness of a sunbeam. Thereupon a voice came out of the midst, " Very right, Mr. Co-operator ; but you have forgotten to read the 15th verse; there stands the main point." A singular incident occurred also during the dispute on Purification. The passage in 2 Maccab. xii. 34, &c., which is usually adduced for this doctrine of the church, was mentioned, and was required to be referred to in the Bible. What was the astonishment of the Protestants, when a learned student sought for this Apocrypha near the book of Joshua! In the meantime, in the handling of such subjects, there was a continual failure through shifts and evasions, while the chief and fundamental doctrines on which the Protestants at the beginning had so urgently insisted, remained altogether undiscussed. An entire afternoon was thus spent in vain: in the evening, the clergy complained of the people's obstinacy, rooted prejudices, want of clearness, &c. "It is, and will remain," they said, "a useless labour to contend with them so long as they retain their own caprices in the interpretation of texts, and will not abandon their private views."

Not much happier effects resulted from the Pastoral Conferences, which in several parishes were held with equal frequency as zeal. In the midst of a Protestant family, for a whole year, no pains were spared to bring them back into the bosom of

the church.   On one occasion, the Vicar declared,
because they would believe nothing but what was
contained in the Bible, that he would shew them a
passage in which the holy Apostle speaks of such
people as they were, and from whence they might
see what, after long patience, ought, in the end, to
be done.   Upon this, he held forth to them the
words, 2 Tim. iii. 1—9.   The owners of the house
kept silence; but one of the neighbours present
remarked, that he also held that chapter in high
respect; that a few weeks ago he had heard it read
in a house at Maierhof, where all had found the
12th verse, and not less verse 14th to the end, to
be very important.   Thereupon, another person
added, that the prophecy occurred to him in which
it is said, "There shall come priests and bishops,
who know not the commandments of God."

A Conference at Hüppach, which lasted several
hours, and at which the people had behaved very
boldly, was concluded by the priest with these
words: "I only wish that the Lord Jesus Christ
himself would come into the room, that I might
say to him, See, these are the people, destroy them
at once, by casting them into hell fire!"   Still
more important was a conversation held by the
parish priest with Bartholomew Heim at Hollen-

zen. Just as the latter had recovered from a severe sickness, the priest came to him one day while he was in the field. "Bartholomew," said he to him, "you look very ill; there is no great while longer for you." "At this moment," as Heim related it, "I felt so strong and well, that I instinctively replied, with a loud voice, God be praised and thanked, Reverend Pastor, it is not yet so bad; the wife and children at home have still too much need of me."

After this, their discourse turned upon the Holy Communion, and on the double form. The pastor repeated emphatically what had formerly been said—"That there is as much contained under one form as under the other, that there can be no body without blood, &c. As the countryman now began to appeal to the Scriptures, the priest remarked, "There is no Bible here, nor is there any need of one." In the meantime they had arrived at the house, where the pastor was requested to stay a while. Heim proposed to continue the discussion by making a careful comparison of Bible texts. The pastor consented, and began by referring to the passage, 1 Samuel, ii. 36, as in favour of the doctrine of only one kind. Heim was of opinion that he did not understand the text aright,

and that when the question regarded the Holy
Communion, it would be better to abide by the
New Testament.   He therefore looked out and
read in succession, Matt. xxvi. 26, John, vi. 54,
1 Cor. xi. &c., according to the text of Luther.
After each passage the ecclesiastic said, " Very
well," and added, when the former had ended,
" Yes, it is even again the old error; you obstinately adhere to what is written, and will hear nothing of the traditions and ordinances of the
church."   *Heim.*   " The church to which I in
heart belong acknowledges Christ as the Law-
giver, and honours his institution of the Supper.
Therefore, also, is it contained in the Augsburg
Confession."   *Priest.*   " It is not proper for thy
wife, and children who still go to school, to be
sitting around while there is a dispute about sacred
things.   Either it must be given up, or we must
go further into another room."   The housekeeper
took up the large Bible under his arm, and, as
there was no other place, conducted the priest into
the kitchen.   On the hearth* he again opened his
book, and with a loud voice read the 10th Article

* The hearths in these countries are built breast high, in the
middle of the rooms.

from the Confession; whereupon the priest said, "There again the proof fails." Heim now was silent a moment, because he did not immediately know what he ought to say. As he kept turning over the leaves, the priest remarked, "When you once get to your books, as I always say. On my coming in, I perceived that the wood was not yet made,* and—" Heim now suddenly exclaimed, "I have it, Reverend Pastor," and recited the 22nd Article "concerning the Communion under both kinds." He might here have mispronounced several Latin names of doctors of the church, which occasioned the priest to say, "It really pains one to hear the holy names so distorted." This, however, did not embarrass Heim, who now came to the words, "Therefore Pope Gelasius himself forbids the Sacrament to be divided." From these he inferred that there was a Papal General Church-Law against the opinion of the ecclesiastic, because he could not read the word "Gelasius," printed in the Roman type,† and so was obliged to

* An expression, the force of which will be perceived by re-membering that these districts abound with wood, and that the people are much employed in felling timber.

† The Germans print only the books written in their own tongue (and not all of these) in the Gothic type, all other languages with the Roman letter.

take the words collectively. Thereupon the priest went away, lamenting over Heim's "very wise want of understanding," while the goodman of the house ran some distance by his side, reading out after him, " Therefore it is not permitted to burden those consciences that desire the Holy Sacrament according to Christ's institution of it, nor to force them to partake it against the ordinance of Christ our Lord."

From this may be seen what credit is due to the reports of the Catholic Journals, when they say, " These people cannot properly be reckoned among any of the acknowledged religious sects; they have but little in common with the peculiar Protestant (Lutheran) Symbols; and even scarcely know the first among the Confessions of that church (the Augsburg Confession) by its name;" and when the same report, partly in contradiction to that just cited, proceeds to make itself merry over the ignorance of these people. "A Clergyman went to a house where none but the ' Awakened' were. He asked them what then properly was their belief. Immediately the mother exclaimed with earnestness, 'We believe in the Holy Trinity, and in the Augsburg Convinion; ' Yes,' repeated two children, ' in the Most Holy Trinity, and the

Augsburg Confiction.' At length the father also observed, 'in the unaltered Augsburg Confession.'"

So far as any attempts to lead them back to the church were exhibited in sermons, they were neither unauthorized, nor, for the pulpit, unsuitable. The author himself has heard several sermons in the Catholic churches of these districts. Polemics were not as of purpose introduced; and even when they did appear, they were not obtruded. Several, especially of the younger clergy, shewed themselves, by their statements and discourses, beyond all expectation to great advantage. Only one sermon contained anything extravagant. This was delivered on a St. Mary's day, when the lecturer took occasion to speak of Spain and Portugal. He vividly described the horrors in those countries—the burning of the monks, the destruction of the churches, the insulting of the nuns, &c., and concluded by declaring, " And all this has been perpetrated by the Protestants, therefore God preserve us from these people; it would be a pretty thing if such were to happen to us." Other particulars relating to this point were communicated by the Protestants themselves. If one of the Separatists attended at a sermon, he was remarked; nor was it uncommon for the preacher immediately to advert to the 'Awakening;' in other instances the presence of such a 'Listener' was pointed out to the congregation. Indeed, the matter did not stop here; invective, mockery, &c., concerning the Protestant church and its dogmas, interchanged with stories about the Reformers, the preachers, their wives, and children, and the like. Such unseasonable controversial discourses must not only have driven the Protestants still further from the church, but, much more, must have caused the weapons to be turned against itself. Of those who remained Catholics, some became fanatics, hatred was excited, and the peace of the neighbourhood disturbed. To others of a better spirit, already stimulated to inquiry, such sermons became as more certain way-marks. The Protestants, however, were by both these manifestations only the more strengthened and confirmed in the truth which they had previously apprehended. "Now is fulfilled," said one of the Protestants, "what the apostle says, 'We have a more sure word of prophecy.' Others have begun to search into the Scriptures, while the priests abused, and the more they clamoured, the more came the people to the Bible."

With regard to their municipal relationships, it

is first and before all others to be observed, that
the disturbances and misunderstandings which occurred in that respect, took place in connexion with
the church, and as a consequence of the dismissal
not having been granted to the Protestants. Whatever the secular power did and ordered in this
behalf was done with reference to the existing
ordinances of the church, or as the executor of the
same. Let us take, first, the case of the marriage-
contract. " Matrimony," so the Catholic Journals
explain the matter, "was refused to them, it is
true," (according to another report, however,
" the case scarcely ever happened,") " and could
not well be otherwise, on the simple ground that
the government does not permit among people
who do not yet belong to any of the tolerated
creeds a merely civil or Protestant contract, at
which the Catholic priest must be present to witness the declaration that the parties take each
other in marriage, and because it is not required of
the Catholic clergy, from regard to their liberty of
conscience, that they, to people who do not, or will
not, belong entirely to the Catholic church, should
give the nuptial blessing."

The next particular to be considered is, their
extra-ecclesiastical assemblies. These had by the

police authorities been partly prohibited and partly
rendered impracticable.   They, in fact, performed
all that the church did and legally could require.
Otherwise it must not be suppressed, that the
Protestants themselves describe this procedure of
the magistracy as a mild one.   It was, for the most
part, only admonitory, never strictly penal.   The
Protestants also express their great satisfaction
that, on the part of the Landgericht, they were not
deprived of their Bibles and other books of edification,* although the authorities knew that they had
such, and were still adding to their store.   On
every occasion, they celebrate in an especial manner the personal treatment they received from
their Landrichter.   "He is the best," said one;
"we would rather a thousand times speak with
him than with the clergy, for he lets one come to
the Word."

* Very different was the conduct of the clergy :—

"A Zillerdaler had obtained from Munich a Catholic New
Testament, a Lutheran Catechism, and several books of devotion which he left at Innsbruck to be bound.   A priest there,
when he heard of this, took them away and sent them back over
the borders.   From the children of a deceased Protestant, a
priest took the Bible and other books of edification left them by
their father, declaring that the deceased had gone to hell, and
that he had said a mass for his soul."—*Appelius.*

On the procedures of the church, also, depended the form and manner of burial among the Protestants. As the clergy would not admit the deceased into the Christian burial-ground, and in general did not at all concern themselves with the subject, it naturally lay upon the magistracy, who could not compel the former, themselves to order and superintend the interment. The practice was this: the Protestants made known the case of death to the local inspector, who sent an official, as the beadle, &c., to the house of mourning. The place of burial was then discussed. If the deceased person had no property, leave was requested to bury him by another Protestant; if this could not be, a piece of common ground, as in a wood, was selected. The policeman attended the funeral, and was rewarded with a florin. In this way the Protestants were protected from those disorders and disturbances which otherwise would have happened. Such protection they thankfully acknowledged; nevertheless, they complained bitterly of the procedure; for at the grave they were never permitted to say aloud any prayers, nor, as they once wished, to sing Luther's Hymn,* and then

* From a Catholic report:—" Of any kind of tender regard for the bodies of the dead they know nothing. They use no prayers on such occasions, and only care to put the corpse

the policeman generally brought his dog with him into the funeral procession. We indeed behold in this, the most simple rights of humanity, in a revolting manner, trampled under foot, but cannot so easily see what was meant by the presence of the dog. Was it intended by the authorities as a sarcasm, or, as the people thought, an intimation of *sepultura canina ?*

Still less intelligible are other ordinances of a purely civil character, which were by the authorities put in operation against these people ; as, for instance, the prohibition against their acquiring any property. Although occasionally certain concessions were made, the matter was yet sufficiently irksome, inasmuch as it lay with the parish to make the decision. They thus became a prey to the caprices, intrigues, and rudeness of individuals, and, unhappily, the clergy did not keep themselves free from such unseemly interferences. More than once, the Pastor of Finkenberg took this method in order to rid his parish of persons inclined to Protestantism. With many also this refusal was attended with other disadvantageous consequences. A youth, on inheriting a freehold,

under ground. Neither do they place any, the least, memorial on the grave, but level it, and let it serve for pasturage as before."

becomes thereby exempt from the conscription. But the inclinant,* John Strasser, "because, on account of his religious principles, he was not qualified to take possession of his estates," was obliged to draw his lots for the conscription; however, he succeeded.

Under this head also may be classed the difficulties which were laid in the way of the Protestants whenever they requested passports. Had these been desired for the purpose of going into a foreign country we could understand the reason of these obstacles. But, against all analogy, we find them employed to prevent the subject from visiting the capital, in order to see the father of his country.

But the more these and other burdens pressed upon the people, the more was their Protestant feeling in its truth and reality manifested. They consoled themselves, suppressing all bitterness, by saying, "Yet much worse befel our Lord; why, then, should we complain?" From such a refined sentiment under oppression, it must be evident that no case occurred of purposed disobedience

* *Inclinant*—a term employed, in a technical sense, to designate those who were *inclined* from the Romish church towards Protestantism.

and resistance to the authorities. At all times, and under all circumstances, they discharged their duty as subjects, and preserved their fidelity and allegiance to the reigning house. Even the last decision, which commanded them to leave their native soil, wrought no alteration in this respect. Nor was it concealed from those among them who possessed the most insight, that the government so acted, as a regard to its circumstances and difficult position rendered unavoidable.

More interesting, however, will it be for our readers to take a glance at the religious state of these people. The author has had an opportunity of becoming acquainted with only a small number of them, and with but a few individuals so intimately as to be able to form a precise judgment concerning them. This, however, is not so difficult with a people so simple, open, and unpractised in any arts of dissimulation.

As one of the ablest, and most penetrated with the character of the gospel, the already-mentioned Bartholomew Heim, of the village of Hollenzen, deserves, undoubtedly, to be distinguished. In him the creative power of God's Word has approved itself in a visible manner. Heim's father was a Catholic, and remained so to the end of his days.

In his youth, Heim was in the service of a rich farmer, in whose house he found Schaitberger's Epistle, which he took with him upon the Alps, and read while keeping his flock. From Schaitberger he went to the Scriptures; afterwards he read Luther's Catechisms; and some years later, the Confession, and other edifying works. Heim shewed a rare acquaintance with every part of the Bible, as also with the Augsburg Confession, an accurate understanding even of difficult passages, a fine clearness in discriminating between essentials and non-essentials. It is undoubtedly due to his discretion that his community were preserved from fanaticism of a prophetical or other kind, which under such circumstances so easily attaches itself.* This will be evidenced by the following

* " Among the Zillerdalers I perceived no appeal to any one as their chief, nor any fanatical opinions indicating a sectarian tendency. On the contrary, they ever sustained their faith by a diligent perusal of the Bible according to Luther's Version, and the older Protestant formularies by which they were guided to the right use of the former. They are also well versed in the Augsburg Confession, which they hold in high esteem. It is not, indeed, to be expected from country people, who, by this method, and without pastoral aid, had embraced the Protestant faith, that they should possess a perfect knowledge and insight in the theological system. Yet it were to be wished that all members of the Protestant church had the words of holy scrip-

incident :—It had been told the author by a bene-
ficed ecclesiastic, that "these people were distinguished by their gross Chiliasm and expectation
of a speedy advent."*   This induced him, on an
occasion when several Protestants were assembled
at Heim's, to ask them, among other questions,
whether they read the Revelation of St. John.
" Why not ?" exclaimed one of those present,
somewhat surprised.   *Heim.* " Thou dost not
understand the gentleman—he has nothing against
the Revelation; and you know well that I have
always said that a man ought to read the New
Testament in the order in which it stands written,
first Matthew, then Mark, &c.   Our gracious God
well knows wherefore it was so given to us."   He

ture so firm in their memories, and so ready for the vindication
of their belief, as the Protestant Zillerdalers with whom I conversed."—Dr. Petri, of Bautzen, in Saxony, who communicated
to the author notes of his visit to the Zillerthal, in August, 1837.

" To my surprise and joy, several individuals shewed an acquaintance with the holy scriptures, and a distinct apprehension
of the passages for the proof of this or that doctrine, which
would ashame many a theologian."—*Appelius.*

* I suppose that the author here refers to attempts to fix
dates, &c., ever the fatal rock to interpreters of prophecy; for
assuredly it is not fanatical and extravagant, but most scriptural
and accordant with the apostolical injunctions, and of the very
essence of the Christian life, not only to be looking for, but even
hastening the coming of the day of God. (2 Peter, iii. 12.)—*Tr.*

afterwards related that some of them had preferred reading in the Revelation, and he had told them that the Apostle Paul must be first understood, otherwise they would not profit. " So," said he, " it happened to me, therefore I know it; with the Apostle Paul lies the kernel. He speaks of the old and new man, of Christ the one Mediator and Intercessor, of the only ground of our salvation, of faith, and justification through faith alone, and not by works, and exercises, and man's wisdom."

When, on a subsequent day, the discourse again turned on the Apocalypse, Heim remarked that the Revelation was too high for him, that he could not bring out all the visions. The author consoled him by saying that the same also happened to learned men. To which Heim replied, " Yet can I not deny that I believe these to be the last days. For what Paul writes, 1 Tim. iv. 1—5, and 2 Tim. iii. 1, &c., is all coming to pass now, and may be seen amongst us." From expressions of this kind it may be that the above-mentioned reproach was framed by evil minds. With what correctness in other respects, and in what sense the Zillerdalers beheld these apostolic words fulfilled in their own experience, the reader himself may judge. We, at least, believe, from the impression which these

E 2

people made on us, that if, when the future lay darkly before them, any crude or unsound notions insinuated themselves, they would be wholly removed when a happier lot should be their portion.

Next to Heim, the mechanic John Fleidl deserves especial attention. He received a Protestant education. His grandfather, whose youth extended to the time of the Saltzburg Persecution, he having died at the age of ninety-eight, was devoted to the gospel. He also possesses an uncommon knowledge of the Holy Scriptures. The texts cited by him he can give in the exact words of Luther's Version, and even with chapter and verse. For other reading, as tracts, &c., he shewed, during his stay in Berlin, little inclination ; he always took the Bible in his hand, or the " Threefold Clover-leaf," which he carried with him on his journeys. Fleidl has a remarkable faculty of discourse, both in speaking and writing, rarely met with among people of his grade, and which Heim himself possesses not. He is also more tranquil and diffident than the latter. Without reason has his way of life been suspected by the adverse party.

These two humble men are they whom we have to contemplate as properly the heads of this Protestant community. Both had, in consequence of their having for a series of years taken the lead in all affairs, won to themselves great respect, and enjoyed a paternal authority over the rest. To this also, in the case of Heim, it contributed not a little that he was the father of a family, and possessed a house of his own. To him the Protestants came to hear whatever was new regarding the affairs of their society, and to ask his counsel in things relating both to the body and the soul. In his house also there was a kind of central library, containing the following books:—1. A Bible in folio, Nürnberg edition, with the Augsburg Confession; 2. Several New Testaments; 3. Luther's Little Catechism, and Collection of Texts, Nürnberg, 1829; 4. Luther's Little Treasury for the New Testament, Stettin, 1738; 5. Federhaff's Fifty-two Bible Histories for home and school; 6. Treasury of Hymns, the Psalm Book of Augsburg; 7. Schmolke's Communion Book, with Morning and Evening Lessons, 1758; 8. The Singing Mouth, a Nürnberg Hymn Book, 1753; 9. Schaitberger's New Evangelical Epistle to the Saltzburgers; 10. The Rose of Prayer and Penitence, 1783; 11. The Heavenly Table of Grace; 12. Büchner's Scripture Concordance; 13. Storr's Confession and Communion Book, fifth edition,

1771; 14. Burk's Little Book for the Communion and Confession, Stuttgart, 1835; 15. Seiler's System of Protestant Doctrine, Erlangen, 1778.

A central library we have called this little collection, as from hence those who belonged to it fetched the books for use, and afterwards carried them back. It was also designed by this arrangement to protect the inexperienced from being misled by improper publications, or such as might be put forward with a jesuitical intention. Other pious writings were also found scattered in several houses; as, for instance, Arndt's True Christianity, and his Sermons; Luther's New Testament, with marginal observations; the Munich Protestant Hymn-book; Hiller's Little Treasury; Spangenberg's Homilies; Muller's Soul's Treasury; Rezendorf's Extract of the Threefold Clover-leaf, (Dreifache Kleeblatt,) containing a history of the Reformation, and of the delivery of the Augsburg Confession. Some fathers of families brought home with them similar works from their journeys. "Yes," said a youth; "our deceased father brought from Suabia, this beautiful book, and we children know it all by heart."

These books also further served for the instruction and cultivation of the youth. It is true, that they were so available only among such as had acquired the elements of reading and writing in the Catholic schools. Since the separation had taken place, the education of the children who were ready for school was undertaken by the elder members of the families, and partly by the parents. But they well perceived that this was an inadequate substitute. "The children learn even nothing at all," said a father. "I would gladly teach them myself, were I not so bad a scholar." Another complained, "This causes me the most pain, that when on a Sunday the children hear us read out of the little book, they always say afterwards, that they also should like to learn." A third, who through the winter had used all his efforts to educate his children, related, that "in the previous spring, when the boys were sent to the meadows to keep the flocks, they began to weep, and said, '.Now we shall never learn any more.'" To which the father replied, "Go forth in God's name; he will instruct you; only be diligent in your prayers."

In former times, those who were inclined to Protestantism were accustomed to hold great meetings, under the guidance and direction of the more advanced and eminent in their community. For the reasons already mentioned, these had latterly been discontinued, so that there remained to them only the service of God in their families. To prevent the evil consequences incidental to such a divided state, some individuals felt strongly impelled to exercise a kind of pastoral care over the others. These visited the brethren, instructed, admonished, warned; and especially brought comfort to the sick and dying. Yet, notwithstanding their extensive influence in this respect, and their deep insight and experience in spiritual subjects, they ever forbore from—what must in their circumstances have been a strong temptation—all intrusion on the sacramental functions. This deprivation of the sacraments was attended with still other evil consequences. Many mothers were offended that their new-born children were brought into the Catholic churches, where none of their own sentiments could be admitted as sponsors, "because it would have endangered the child's salvation if a Lutheran had been its godfather." Add to this, it frequently occurred that as many of the Catholics refused, it being against their conscience, one of the clergy resolved at last to undertake the office. In former years, several had expressed doubts as to the validity of such a baptism, which ceased, however, when the initiated had explained what was essential to it.* Still more critical was the matter: with regard to the holy sacrament of the altar. That they could not partake of it in the Catholic church is evident; since, in order to this, they must first have purged themselves by penance, and have submitted to the withholding of the cup, which had always been to them an especial grievance. Bnt even if they had so desired, it would not have been possible, as they would thus have declared their return to the church, and been involved in further consequences that would not have failed to follow. The want of this sacrament was indeed acutely felt by many, especially by females, the aged, and the sick. Their complaints at the season of Easter, when all the people flock to the communion, were loud, and caused much grief and anxiety to their leaders and the heads of families. The embarrassment was greatest when the dying languished for this last consolation. Nevertheless, there occurred among them no contempt of the

* In order the more firmly to attach the baptized to the church, and to render their departure from it more difficult, every means was resorted to, to bring the children to confirmation; not unfrequently by persuading the mothers, bribing the relations, &c. Contrary to the custom of the church, this rite was administered to infants before they were a month old.

visible sacrament, after the manner of the pseudo-mystics;* still less, as their adversaries admit, any self-willed administration of the sacred office. "No man shall administer the sacrament without a regular call," they said, with a knowledge as accurate, as their observance was conscientious, of the Augsburg Confession. (Art. 14.)

Under these circumstances, among all the wishes expressed by these people, that for a regular church and school system was the loudest and most urgent. When asked, whether they could support a clergyman and schoolmaster, they replied, "Why not? Butter, and cheese, and bread, he shall have as much as he needs; we can also build him a little house; but indeed we have not much money."

* Even the Catholic journals acknowledge, "There was in no instance any the least trace of a false mysticism among the people."

CHAPTER III.

Moral and social life of the Zillerdalers—Reproaches and accusations of their enemies—Strifes and provocations between
the parties—Indifference to religion among the Catholics—
Humble confession of the Protestants.

WITH respect now to the moral and social life of
these people, there were not wanting, as may be
supposed, reproaches of the most various kinds
from the opposite party. They were charged with
having in many ways offended against both civil
and ecclesiastical order, and also against the
general morality. Accusations of the former kind,
the Catholic journals report in a more general
way. Thus they say—" They derided the mys-
teries of the Catholic religion, disturbed processions, crucifixes and images openly profaned,
heaped insults against the Catholics and their
priests, and even threatened them with death ; the

tokens of the Catholic church, which their children received from the priests, they trod under
foot; at home, in the presence of their Catholic
servants, they read to their children the most
violent of the Protestant controversial writings,
those edifying books which they had brought
with them from abroad, laughing out aloud at
the passages which contained the coarsest invec-
tives against the Catholic church, and exclaim-
ing to the reader, 'That is fine, read that again.'
They said, when any one, in order not to be a
partaker in others' sins, called the attention of
his priest to what occurred in such houses, that he
was a 'parson's beadle;' and if any female in such
a house or neighbourhood refused to coincide in
their revilings, but behaved quietly, and diligently
attended church, that she was a 'parson's wife.'"

For the forming of a right judgment on such accusations, one finds a hint in these reports themselves, as they acknowledge that "such calumnies
were wholly disapproved of by other members of
the sect;" thus making the same distinction which
has been already occasionally intimated.*   Not all

* " In general, the impression made upon me by these people was, that they were of a vigorous, powerful, and discerning
nature; that if sanctified by grace, and duly initiated in the

those inclined to Protestantism observed, indeed, that quietness and moderation, that propriety of demeanour and foresight, which were evinced by the individuals who have been before described. Many suffered themselves to be carried away by their forward and vehement zeal against the gaudy appendages of the Catholic worship. This occurred more frequently in the earlier years, and with many, who neither by a Protestant education nor intercourse had been humanized, not seldom bordered upon rudeness. Unhappily, inconvenient discussions relating to religion and the church occurred, which were carried on without becoming prudence, and were even sought after, to the abandonment of all discretion and propriety. Whenever they happened on public occasions, as in taverns, &c., they almost invariably led to bad results. Men irritated and provoked one another, took opposite sides, and both Catholics and Protestants employed a coarse expression,* which is

spirit of the gospel, they would be capable of great achievements. For the present, among many, especially the youth, a polemical anti-Catholic tendency appeared to predominate, which in their situation is very natural."—*Voelter.*

* Even the better and more earnest among the Protestants employed the phrase " gluttonous parson," as a common form of speech, without intending anything especially offensive.

natural to the Tyrolese. The news of such events ran rapidly through the valley. That there were much perversion and distortion of the real facts will surprise no one. A case, the report of which was attended by many consequences, was thus related by a person of undoubted veracity—A smith, Joseph Hohenleitner by name, went one day to Maierhof for the purposes of his occupation. While he was drinking a glass of beer in an ale-house, a priest passed by, carrying the holy communion to a person that was sick. Several Catholics who were present left the room and went into the street, falling on their knees, according to their custom, in order to receive the priest's blessing. Hohenleitner, however, kept his seat. Thereupon, one asked him, why he also did not go. Others were more urgent, until at last he broke out with these words, " I am not going to that Baal's work." For this expression he was afterwards condemned to eighteen weeks' imprisonment at Rattenberg; since which period he has been sickly, as the water of that place is said not to agree with the Zillerdalers.

Contentions of this nature occurred very frequently, especially since such wonderful things happened in the country, which were told the people by the priests in their sermons, and adduced in proof of their religion. Such, for instance, were the story of the Holy Maid of Caldera,* the miracle at the bone-house of Zell;† and, lastly, the report of a dead body recomposed from the bones in the catacombs, that was sent by the holy father to an inhabitant of Zillerthal.

The Catholic journals also contain other criminations against the social and moral conduct of the Protestants. The author willingly declines the task of investigating and discussing all such accusations, for the purpose of being able to refute them. Many of them are so general and undefined, that a minute acquaintance with localities

---

* The holy maid of Kaldern is properly a young lady named Maria von Moerl, of Kaldern, in Etschthal. Her visions and ecstasies have many things in common with those of the devout Anna Catharina von Emmerich, at Dülmen. Every Thursday at noon she suffers the agony in the garden; on Friday morning she accompanies Jesus on his path of suffering, expiring at mid-day in the most violent convulsions; on Christmas and Epiphany she is in the train of shepherds, kings, &c. At the season of her transformations, she hovers, with hands folded, over her bed, bears in her hands the marks of the wounds, which on Friday evening gush forth. She is in her twenty-fourth year, and for three years has taken scarcely any food.

† A withered lily in the hand of the Virgin's image at that place, which suddenly put forth new blossoms.

and statistical details would be requisite in order to arrive at any certainty; others, again, are so special, that a complete investigation by examinations, confrontations, &c., would be necessary; and, after all, it might appear doubtful whether the facts could be truly ascertained, especially if relating to events long since past.

Among the accusations of this class may be reckoned the following report, contained in the Catholic journals:—"Scandalous," says the Journal for Catholic Theology, "is their course of life; illegitimate births happen very frequently among them; and it is a common occurrence for them to live together in contempt of the marriage bond, and by their corrupting example to mislead the thoughtless youth." It is, however, remarkable that "The Catholic," which otherwise omits nothing prejudicial in its description of the Protestants, says nothing of such an especial irregularity; nor is it less surprising that the Catholic inhabitants of the valley are ignorant of such flagrant offences. At the same time, it cannot be denied that there were instances among the Protestants of children being born out of wedlock: this they themselves have admitted, referring, as some palliation, to the refusal of the rite of marriage. A case, concerning which the Journal for Catholic Theology says, " It is one unknown even among the heathen," resolves itself, to the astonishment of the reader, into this, that a man from Ramsberg, on account of a misdemeanour committed while in a state of inebriation, had suffered fourteen days' imprisonment. When this story is accompanied by " The Catholic" with the fine phrase, " Such uncivilized men the little enlightened church carries in its bosom," it is to be remembered that the Protestants at no time rejoiced in such an acquisition.

To all these movements against the Catholic Church, the religious indifference among the Catholics themselves, as we have already noticed, forms the dark back-ground. "It is no wonder" —such was the expression of one of this tendency —"that the people (the Protestants) run away from the belief and practice of things which are no longer to be believed in the present day." Yet to join themselves to the Protestants was far enough from the design of these daring spirits. "What folly so to rack one's brains with fanaticism and prayers, and the everlasting reading of little books!" For expressions of this nature, the Protestants had not unfrequently to answer, as when

F

the Catholic journals report that "One who had passed for a great light, and had turned many to his views, said to a Catholic, 'I have read the Holy Scriptures from my youth, yet have I found nothing therein concerning the Godhead of Jesus, and that men should pay him adoration, nor concerning his presence in the Eucharist; you are only adorers of bread and idol-worshippers.'" That men of such a purely negative way of thinking should, by common report, be classed among the Protestants, may be easily conceived. Among these, however, at least such as formed the main body, not the slightest trace has been met with by the author. They have, from the beginning, with their guides and leaders, belonged to quite another school. With wonderful delicacy of the moral sense, they at all times perceived, and openly acknowledged, in how many things they were still deficient, being in this respect much more keen-sighted than even their enemies. Thus, with grief, they confessed to the author, that during this course of years many things had taken place which ought not to have occurred, and which were especially unbecoming in Protestant Christians. Not only have they lamented over the above-mentioned points, but also over their negligence in spiritual matters, over the fear of man which had kept so many, from avowing their profession,* and their actual denial of known truth.† All, it was their opinion, would have happened far otherwise, and more favourably, had they been able to attain a regular church communion; that rather one must wonder that no worse evil had befallen them, nor "can they sufficiently thank God, who hitherto has holpen them by preserving their minds one towards another, and preventing them by His grace from so many dangers."

* "They told me that there were numbers who only feigned being Catholics, but who would immediately fall away on their attaining liberty of faith, held back by the dread of losing their worldly substance, and of incurring the animosity of the priests, by which their life would have been embittered."—*Appelius.*

"They assured us that there were many in the Tyrol secretly inclined to Protestantism, as the Protestant leaven could never be wholly extirpated."—*Voelter.*

† Appelius mentions several cases of betrothed persons not being able to obtain a legitimate marriage, except by returning to the Church, and depositing a sum of money as a pledge for their fidelity.

CHAPTER IV.

Situation of the Protestants of Zillerthal with relation to other countries—Fleidl's letter to his friends in Bavaria—Visits of their brethren in the faith to the valley—Intercourse with Munich—Fleidl is deputed to Berlin, and addresses the King—Audience of the deputy—Admission into the Prussian dominions.

THE circumstances and situation of the Protestants in Zillerthal had been, in the main points, for several years, not entirely unknown in other countries. Early in the year 1837, Fleidl communicated the following letter, which he sent to some friends in Bavaria.*

" Most worthy Friends and Brethren in the Lord,

" We, your Protestant brethren in Zillerthal, inform you of the situation in which we are at pre-

---

* Quarterly Review, vol. lxiv. p. 131.

ent placed, and of which we were not aware when we sent to you Joseph Gruber. The matter stands thus : On the 12th of March the district-captain came to Zillerthal, and summoned us all, the first on the 13th and the last on the 17th of March, to appear before him, and we did so with all due obedience. Thereupon he stood up, and said that to-day he appeared not as district-captain, but as the Emperor himself, to declare to us the Imperial decision of January 11, 1837, as to the following points :—

" 1st. That we must return to the Roman Catholic Church, or leave our fatherland ; that he will not tolerate any Protestant community in the Tyrol.

" 2nd. That we might have the choice either to be translocated into Austrian provinces, where there are Protestant congregations, or to emigrate into foreign parts.

" 3rd. That we must declare within fourteen days which we prefer.

" 4th. That from the date of our declaration, a term of four months should be granted us to prepare for translocation or emigration.

" 5th. If in four months ye are not ready for either one or the other, your freedom of choice will be at an end, the official authorities will summon you to move, and the Emperor will locate you where he pleases.

"Thereupon we requested passports, that we might look about for some place to go to; to which the answer was,—' When you have made your declaration you shall have passports, but not before.' We then considered, from all that we knew of old, and that we had just heard, that our brethren in the faith suffer oppression in Austria. We thought also of the 30,000 Saltzburgers; who, for religion's sake, were obliged to tread the same path, and how the King of Prussia graciously received them. We have heard that the present King too is a good and a pious King, and a friend of the Protestant Church ; and so, excepting eight persons who go into Austria, we ventured, in dependence upon God and the good King, to declare for foreign parts. Many now declared, of whom we knew nothing before : the number of those who have declared for emigration is between 400 and 500 souls, and we intended, as soon as we could get a passport, to send one of the number to Prussia to pray and secure a gracious reception for all. But now they refuse the passport, and we do not know what is to be the end of it.

"Now we remember the 5th point, which says,
'If you are not ready within this term, the Emperor
will locate you,' and think that they delay with
the passport that the time may pass away, and so
the last state be worse than the first. We therefore pray you one and all, most worthy friends, to
intercede for us with the King, and to inform him
of our condition; and as soon as one of us can get
a passport, he shall go himself to Prussia, and we
will look for you to give us information: but, should
it happen that they will not give us a passport to
Prussia, inform the bearer whether he could not
enter Prussia with his labourer's passport: he will
return home at Whitsuntide. If it be possible for
this man with his labourer's passport to get into
Bavaria and Prussia, we should wish to send him.
If we only knew that the King of Prussia would
receive us, we would serve him faithfully and up-
rightly, as we have hitherto served the Emperor,
who now persecutes us and drives us from our
fatherland.

"We greet you one and all, and pray for all
things possible.

"JOHN FLEIDL."

In Munich especially, the state of things was
pretty accurately understood. Zillerdalers who
trafficked with precious stones, and such like
articles, were in the constant habit of going ,to
and from that city. They were treated by several
of their brethren with that reception which Christian love is ever accustomed to grant to the needy
and oppressed. Yet were there no attempts at
proselytizing; for the new-comers were already
acquainted with the Gospel, and rejoiced in the
opportunity of uniting with Protestants in the
public worship of God, the holy sacraments, &c.
In like manner the Zillerdalers received visits of
sympathy from their fellow-believers in Bavaria
and other places.* The Austrian policy permitted
this, and, even when it might have had ground
for interference, it placed no difficulties in the

---

* Unfortunately, freebooters and other worthless characters,
under the assumed name of Protestants, also paid them visits.
One of these, pretending to have come from Russia in the spring
of 1835, made known to Heim his pecuniary embarrassments.
The latter offered him the greatest part of his ready money;
but as this was asserted not to be sufficient, Heim borrowed of
his brother-in-law. In this way he was beguiled of twelve
crowns, with the promise that they should be returned by the
next St. James' day. A similar case occurred again in the
following year.

way.*· 'Now, after the decision already mentioned had been made known to these Zillerdalers, and they·had been joined by a hundred and twenty-two other inhabitants of the valley, they appointed John'·Fleidl their deputy, who, on behalf of the Protestants, should look around for help, and seek a reception in a foreign country. As the granting of his·passport was delayed for some months, so that nearly half of the allotted term had passed away, they obtained, upon petition, a prolongation of their sojourn until the 11th of September. At the end of May, Fleidl appeared in Berlin, and delivered to the King the following address, drawn up chiefly by himself:—†

* The ordinance mentioned by Voelter, that "not only travellers who remained over night, but such as only stopped an hour, should enter their names in the stranger's book," was not in existence till after the year 1836.

† "The good King of Prussia had, however, heard already the tidings of this oppression in Austria; and another good King, our own late Sovereign, had heard also the tale of cruelty and injustice. To the eternal honour of William IV. be it recorded, that he was the first who moved in the matter. Again and again, in February and March, 1837, he called upon the King of Prussia to interfere. They had both been parties to the Act of Confederation—they had both guaranteed its observance: they could not see its provisions trampled under foot, to the oppression and ruin of the Protestants of the Tyrol, without sacrificing every principle of self-respect, humanity, veracity,

"To the most Illustrious, most mighty King.

"Most Gracious King and Lord,

"In my own name, and in the name of my companions in the faith, whose number amounts to from 430 to 440, I venture a cry of distress on the magnanimity and grace of your Majesty, as the august defender of the pure Gospel. With my whole soul I had desired to lay this prayer

honour, and religion. The King of England and Hanover found no want of sympathy on the part of his Prussian brother, a worthy descendant of those sovereigns who opened their arms to receive the victims of Popery flying from France, from Saltzburg, and Bohemia. He was as determined as King William, but desired to act as gently as possible to the Emperor of Austria; and therefore, instead of adopting the form of diplomatic reclamation, which must have been attended with a public exposure of political delinquency and breach of faith, he quietly commissioned his chaplain, Dr. Strauss, who was going to Vienna, to intercede with Prince Metternich, that, to such families as preferred emigration into Prussia, permission and time for preparation might be granted, as he was willing to receive them all. A revocation or alteration of the decree of banishment was not asked for—for this reason amongst others, that a longer stay in the Tyrol under such circumstances could not have been desirable to the Protestants themselves. In fact, immediately after the departure of the King's chaplain from Berlin, on the 23rd of May, 1837, the Zillerdalian deputy to the King of Prussia arrived to solicit a quiet habitation for the victims of intolerance: this was the already mentioned John Fleidl."—Quarterly Review, vol. lxiv. pp. 132, 133.

personally and orally before your Majesty, yet I am content, if permitted, to do so only in writing. After more than a hundred years, another act of persecution and banishment has been repeated in our fatherland. Not for any crimes or misdemeanours on our part, but on account of our religion, we are compelled to leave our native soil, as the annexed certificate from the Landgericht of Zell, dated 11th of this month, will shew. It is true that we have the choice between a translocation into another Austrian province and an entire emigration; but we prefer the latter, in order to spare ourselves and children all further animosities. Already once, Prussia gave to our persecuted forefathers a secure asylum. We, too, have placed all our trust in God and the good King of Prussia. We shall find help, and not be ashamed. We therefore most humbly beseech your Majesty for a favourable reception into your royal dominions, and for a gracious assistance on our settlement. We pray your Majesty to receive us paternally, that so we may live according to our faith. Our belief is grounded entirely on the doctrine of Holy Scripture and the Augsburg Confession; we have read both with diligence, and well know the difference between the Word of God and man's additions. From this faith we neither can nor will ever deviate; for its sake we leave house and home, and also our fatherland. May your Majesty graciously permit us to remain together in one community; that will increase our mutual help, our mutual comfort. May your Majesty graciously place us in a region whose circumstances have some resemblance to our own Alpine land; wherein agriculture, and the rearing of cattle, have formed our occupations. About two-thirds of us have property; a third support themselves by day-labour; only eighteen are tradespeople, of whom thirteen are weavers.

"May it please your Majesty to give us a faithful pastor, and a zealous schoolmaster, though at first we shall probably not be in a condition to afford much for their support. The journey will be very expensive, and we do not yet know what we shall be able to bring to our new home; and we have long been deprived of the consolations of religion and school instruction. Should any want shew itself among us, especially among the poor, to whom the more opulent may not be able to give sufficient assistance, as they will be obliged to begin life anew, so may your Majesty be a father to us all. But especially will your Majesty graciously intercede for us, that the prescribed term of four months, from the 11th of May to the 11th of September, may be prolonged till the next spring? The sale of our farms, which already has begun, but which cannot, in so short a time, be well ended without disadvantage; the setting in of winter; the helplessness of the old people and children, are considerations which make such a prolongation in the highest degree desirable. May God reward your Majesty for all the kindness which your Majesty may shew to us. Faithful, honest, and thankful, will we remain in Prussia, and will not lay aside the good qualities of our Tyrolese nature. We shall only increase the number of your Majesty's brave subjects, and stand in history as a lasting monument, that misfortune, when it dwells near compassion, ceases to be misfortune; and that the Gospel, when obliged to fly from the Papacy, ever finds protection from the magnanimous King of Prussia.

"THE TYROLESE OF ZILLERTHAL,

"By their spokesman,

"JOHN FLEIDL, of Zillerthal.

"Berlin, 27th May, 1837."

The petitioner was graciously received in the highest quarters, and his suit was answered to the entire satisfaction both of the deputy and his constituents. The King declared himself ready to accede to the request in its full extent; which he, in his own name and in that of his associates, had presented, with the knowledge and consent of his country's government.

At the same time that Fleidl was gone to Berlin, the government had repeatedly received authentic information respecting the affairs of the Ziller-dalers. Dr. Strauss,* the president of the Consistory, was, in consequence, sent to Vienna, in order to negotiate the particulars, and to request for them a prolongation of the term for their emigration; in which application he was successful. The Austrian government acceded, with all readiness, to the proposals of the Prussian, shewing a disposition to avoid everything that might give to the affair the odious colour of a religious persecution. Dr. Strauss met deputies from Zillerthal at Kreuth. There he ascertained that their faith was in strict accordance with the principles of

* Carefully to be distinguished from D. F. Strauss, author of the too celebrated neological work entitled " The Life of Jesus Christ."

Scripture and the Church, and that they were desirous to, unite themselves as well to the Protestant Church as to all the institutions therewith connected. Subsequently, the privy-councillor Jacobi was commissioned to acquaint them with the civil institutions of the state, that so no circumstance, as that of the general military duty, might come upon them unawares.

The news of these transactions awakened great joy among the Protestants. They immediately set about preparing for their emigration, by building wagons for their journey, disposing of their houses, estates, &c. The majority of those who had farms, and other property, soon found good and profitable purchasers. The others, also, who possessed only houses and cattle, were in no embarrassment, as all kinds of saleable commodities find in the valley a ready purchase.* The officials were not negligent in laying before them the

* That an assurance upon oath was required of the purchasers, "that they would never more betake themselves to the Bible," is a mistake, and originated probably from the circumstance that married persons, children, and members of families who remained behind, were compelled to swear that " they would never know anything more of those who were taking their departure." This custom is indeed nothing new ; it occurred, with more oppressive conditions, in the time of Count Firmian.

hypothecary books, in order that the emigrants
might have security upon the property of the
buyers.   But the Protestants declared that they
were not disposed to make sales of that kind;
that indeed, for them, their countrymen were of
themselves sufficient security.   It was in vain that
Schlechter, their landrichter, explained to them
the advantages of this right; they remained by
their declaration.   Neither did the government
require of them the emigration tax, but furnished
the poorest among them with the necessary means
for their journey.

CHAPTER V.

The emigration from Zillerthal—Preparations for departure—
Disposition and behaviour of those who remained in the
valley—March of the Exiles through the country above the
town of Ems—Their reception by the Protestants in Rut-
zenmoos and Efferding—Parting scenes in Finkenberg—
Opinions of the Catholics concerning the Exiles—Their per-
formance of divine worship on the mountains—Meeting of
the emigrants with a priest—Their reception by the Protestants at Thenning and Gallneukirchen, and scornful
treatment at Iglau.

FOURTEEN days earlier than the expiration of the
set term, they began their departure. Their parting from those whom they left in the valley must
have been so much the more bitter, as even many
who had hitherto been their enemies, moved with
sympathy, now declared that " they never thought
their opposition would have led to such a sad
result; that they only intended to effect a change
in their resolution." Others also, of a more in-

G

different character, assumed towards them a milder tone, especially since they had taken the pains to acquaint themselves more precisely with the facts. Urgent were the entreaties that "they yet would remain in the valley, lest otherwise they should cause a scandal to the people abroad; what would be said in the empire about the Tyrolese?" It was probably from similar feelings that some were induced to promise their relations and acquaintance worldly advantages, if they would stay in the valley and remain by the Church. The family of L——, with seven children, had packed up their scanty effects upon a small cart, which, in the evening, was standing before the door, ready to depart the next morning. At this moment a female relative came and offered the husband the freehold of a rich farm, if he would consent to adhere to the Church. "I do not sell my religion," he calmly replied. Some priests also performed their part, for the purpose of directing attention and sympathy to the Exiles: but they did it in their own way. On the borders of the valley of Kützen, one chose for the subject of his discourse "the judgment of God upon the Luthe-rans;" in which he alleged, "It is too bad that the people should be allowed to take so much

money with them as two hundred thousand imperial florins;* however, they will need the greater
part on their journey, and the remainder will soon
be gone. But, my hearers," he continued, " Prussia
is a poor country; the means of life are all dear
there; even mouse-flesh is sold for money, &c."
Notwithstanding, the Exiles experienced much
kindness on their way. In Maierhof many came
forward to give them a friendly farewell, and to
express their sorrow " that matters had come to
such a pass." Even in Catholic Fügen, females
stood under their houses weeping at their departure, and presented, unasked, refreshments to
the women and children.

According to the wish of the Austrian Government, they took their way through the Imperial
States, Saltzburg, the Archduchy, Moravia, and
Bohemia; and in small divisions. The first, consisting of one hundred and fifty souls, passed, on
the 7th of September, through Linz. Some of
the more advanced, availed themselves of the op-

---

* " The fact is, that they brought into Prussia 50,000 reichs-
dollars, and about as much more remained due to them in their
native valley. This sermon, however, shews that the impression
on their Romanist neighbours was not, that want had compelled
them to emigrate."—Quarterly Review, vol. lxiv. p. 136.

portunity to visit a Protestant weekly service at Wels. No sooner had the congregation at Rützenmoos heard that a second division was to follow, than they sent deputies on the high road as far as Boeklabrug to meet the Emigrants, and to invite them to take up their quarters with them for the night, and to attend divine service on the 8th of September, the festival of the Nativity of the Virgin. Here many, for the first time, entered a Protestant church. Pastor Trautberger preached on the twenty-third Psalm, commencing his discourse with the words, "This day is salvation come to my house." Immediately after, the commissary of the march directed them to proceed forward over Maria-Scherten. This train was more considerable than the first, consisting of two hundred persons. Every two or three families had, in common, a wagon drawn by horses. Many of the poorer dragged along a small two-wheeled cart, carrying their goods and children. In this manner Fleidl conveyed his mother and four little children. On the Saturday they arrived in Wels and in Scharten, the seat of the Protestant superintendent; where the inhabitants opened their houses to them, and where also, for the first time, they met with unkindness from the adverse party.

Even a priest suffered himself to do them this wrong. After accosting the Zillerdalers with a certain show of kindness, he proceeded to harsh words, and concluded: " Now you are going to the place you belong to, even the desolate Riesengebirg; few of you, however, will arrive there, most will perish on the way through Bohemia." " That does not trouble us," replied an artisan; " if we live, we live to the Lord, and if we die, we die to the Lord." On Sunday, the 10th of September, they distributed themselves in the chapels (Bethäuser) at Scharten, Wallen, and Efferding; but the greater number remained at Efferding.

There the congregation devoted the front seats around the altar to the strangers. The service began with the hymn,

> " Chiist says, Come, follow me," &c.

After this, Pastor Kotschy commenced his discourse with those lines of Terstegen's:—

> " Forget not God's free grace and love,
> Nor from Him e'er depart;
> While many thousands harden'd prove,
> His mercy won thy heart."

He then acquainted the congregation with the fortunes of the Zillerdalers, and strikingly reminded them of the banishment, a century before, of the Saltzburgers, who then sang,

> " A wandering exile here I roam,
>   No other name is mine;
> For God's truth driv'n from land and home:
>   Yet I will not repine,
> Since Thou, my Saviour, didst for me
>   The path of grief not shun;
> So that I may but follow Thee,
>   Let all Thy will be done."*

The sermon was founded especially on the epistle for the day, Ephesians iii. 13, &c. After which the congregation sang the hymn, commencing

> " Glory and praise to God most High."

This ended, there followed a baptism, then a confession, and the holy eucharist.   As it was all

---

* As the original is in the Tyrolese dialect, which differs from the High German, I thought it would be an interesting specimen to some readers.

> " I bin a armer Exulant
>   A so thue i mi schreiba,
> Ma,thuet mi aus em Vaterland
>   Um Gottes Wort vertreiba,
> Dess weiss i wohl Herr Jesu Christ
>   Es ist dir au so ganga,
> Itzt will i dein Nachfolger sin
>   Herr, machs nach dein verlanga."—*Tr.*

new·to the Tyrolese, they remained silent spectators in the church.

At noon they were hospitably entertained by
the members of the congregation. Many now,
lifting up their hearts and voices, said, " God be
thanked, it has happened quite otherwise than was
foretold us. It was said, ' If indeed you reach
Hausrück, no one will regard you as fellow-believers. They will sweep you out as with a besom,
and, least of all, will permit you to enter their
chapels.' "

In the afternoon, they attended the catechising
of the children, which that day was held on the
41st chapter of the book of Genesis. To this the
pastor added, with reference to the case of the
Emigrants, a discourse on the 11th verse of the
8th chapter of the Prophecy of Amos. At the
conclusion, he directed his address especially to
them, admonished them to be faithful, and, com-
mending them to the divine protection, imparted
to them the blessing. Afterwards, several of them
visited the clergyman at his own house, conversed
with him on several passages of Scripture, and expressed their thankfulness at the wonderful lead-
ings of God's providence. Especially joyful were

a blind old man of eighty-three years, and a still more aged widow, for having lived to attain the privilege of worshipping their Lord in a Protestant church, and hearing his word without distraction. The Protestant congregations also afforded the travellers considerable assistance in all things necessary for their journey.

On the same day a third division, consisting of sixty persons, arrived from the Lower Innthal, on the high road to Reichenhall. With several of these the fore-mentioned clergyman from Franconia had been already acquainted in the valley. "I found in Finkenberg," he writes, " Q——, and his family busily occupied in preparing for their emigration. A deeply interesting picture! The man with his brothers was standing in the entrance, filling baskets for the journey. The gray-headed father was within the house, surveying with a keen eye every corner of the place still so dear to him, lest anything should be forgotten. The wife, with an infant eight days old at her breast, was, with Christian resignation, sitting by a cradle wherein a sick boy was lying. At the door stood the sister in tears, lamenting the separation from her kindred, whom she would gladly have accompanied, had she not been held back by her love to the children of her rigidly Catholic husband.

"They invited me to their noonday meal, the last they were to partake of in the paternal home. At table, the father of the family—of whom I may not think it evil that he did not bear this trial with the patience of his Lord—confessed that ' he felt the flesh still to struggle against the spirit; but,' he added, ' I hope, by God's help, it will soon be overcome.' Among other questions, I asked him if he was going to take his religious books with him, as the Bible, Schaitberger's Epistle, &c., or whether he had sold them. He replied, smiling, ' I do not sell the Word of God, that I have bestowed upon people by whom it will be duly valued, as others also have done, because many have earnestly besought us to leave them some of our little books. Besides, the good king will not fail to give us others when we arrive in Prussia.' The next day I proceeded on the Saltzburg road as far as Rattenberg. Here, among the inhabitants, I met with various—some of them strange— opinions concerning the Zillerdalers. One man insisted, that the people were desirous of becoming Jews; on my asking why, he replied, ' because they do not make the sign of the cross in' their prayers, which the Jews also refuse to do.' 'The hostess of the brewery at Wiesgrund thus expressed her opinion: 'I should only like to know what really is the matter with these poor mad people. I know them to be honest and industrious;' they have also wished to give my husband some little books, but as he cannot read, he is not able to make any use of them. It is true, they lead a temperate and sober life, only they are not right in their religion, for they do not believe in the mother of God; and yet they are stricter than most of us in their honour of the Lord.' An apprentice asserted that they were deserving of all praise, only their inclination to Protestantism was bad. In Rattenberg the conversation was entirely devoted to this affair. As one was here relating the hardships of the journey, of the children, and of the country to which they were going, another remarked, 'It is much better to remain in the religion in which one has been brought up.' Another person from 'Achenthal said, 'The novices! they wish to be wiser than the Church, and only seek to make themselves conspicuous.' To which a third added, "The matter has also its other side; the people have

heard, something which they do not understand;
they are too early with it yet.' Very interesting
was the expression of a traveller from Pustherthal,
who, as it seemed, was not unacquainted with the
Word of God. 'In my country,' said he, 'many
think just as these wanderers do; but it is best for
a man to remain quiet.' After passing the village
of St. John, I accompanied them further on the
road. The clear tones of the bells from the mountains were summoning the dwellers in the valley
to devotion. In festal dress, the old and young
were hastening by us to the neighbouring churches.
It was the Lord's Day, and the Emigrants felt
much anxiety that they, by their journeying,
should disturb the Sunday's rest, and that themselves could not enjoy the happiness of hearing the
Word of God. I endeavoured to calm their ap-
prehensions as to the first point, and expressed my
readiness to do my part for the general edification.
At a green spot, in the wild mountain pass over
the immense snow-crowned glaciers, they all de-
scended from the wagons, and encamped around.
I stepped into their midst, and discoursed to them,
choosing for the subject the words in Matthew,
v. 10—12. At the conclusion, they sang a choral,

which reverberated with a magnificent echo from
the surrounding valleys. Some hours later we
arrived at Waidring, and the pass of Strub. It
was just at the time when, the mass being ended,
the people were returning to their homes. The
sight of the procession caused them almost all to
halt, and, either with sympathy or curiosity, to
direct their eyes upon the people. Soon, however,
the construction of the travelling wagons and the
like alone attracted their attention; especially as
a priest joined himself to the bystanders, and
charmed all with the displays of his technical
knowledge. He also spoke freely concerning the
' Inclinants,' confidently maintaining, that ' these
people, in order to procure a more favourable reception in Prussia, had told lies to its ruler, pro-
fessing to believe in the Augsburg Confession, 'of
which, all the while, they knew but little, and
understood still less.' As I hereupon called him
to account, and demanded of him proof for these
assertions, he turned away, and poured forth a
series of reproaches against a nobleman, who, in
this district, had lately separated from the Catholic
Church. On our way, a countryman came up
with us. He had remarked nothing of the sermon,

except that it had stated that the Lutherans, were really, heathens, and deniers of the Godhead. I gave him Schubert's excellent little work, 'The History of the Lutheran Saltzburgers;' which he received with joy, promising me, that one of his children should read it to him in the afternoon.

" At noon we reached the valley watered by the Salach, and enclosed by the bare chalk mountains; then we re-ascended the heights towards the Kniepass, and arrived at the frontier village of Unken, celebrated as the scene of a murderous battle in the year 1809. On the road, my companion Q—— related to me several particulars of his early life in the valley. Among other incidents the following: ' On one occasion my pastor blamed me very harshly for presuming to read the Bible, whereas, as he said, it belongs only to God's servants, the priests. He did not suffer me to appeal to the Word, but continued to represent this as our chief crime. At length I ventured to say, ' Reverend pastor, I have read the Scripture, and that often, yet have I not been able to find that it anywhere is said to be only for the clerical order. There is indeed the Epistle of St. Paul to the *Church* at Rome, at Corinth, &c. The *Church* at

Rome certainly consisted then of the people 'in general, and if, at that period, they were permitted to read the Scripture, they must be equally so at the present day.'

" Among the Emigrants were two sisters who had joined one of their relatives, leaving the rest of the family at home with their father, who was sick. On my asking them whether they thought it right so to forsake their invalid father for ever, they replied, ' Yes, for had he been well, he would have come with us, and at parting, he gave us his blessing for the journey.' "

On the thirteenth of the same month, this third division arrived at Wels, and attended a lecture on the twenty-seventh Psalm, by the Protestant clergyman of that place. Pursuing their journey, they came to Thenning. There the Lutheran superintendent received them with especial kindness, and induced them to remain over the Sunday. In Linz they found a hospitable reception, and accommodation gratis at the Golden Cross. In Gallneu-kirchen, where formerly the beloved Boos laboured, the parish priest forbade his flock to have anything to do with the people. Nevertheless, the commissary of the district opened to them his stables, and his example was followed by several others. Many now were the marks of sympathy shewn to them, until they reached the borders of the Archduchy. These were, however, strikingly diminished on their arrival in Moravia. Here, in several places, difficulties arose from the difference of dialect, which the inhabitants shewed no disposition to obviate, but rather a decided aversion to the Exiles. The first train, especially, probably in consequence of their strange and unexpected appearance, had to endure many hardships.

In the hill town of Iglau, their leaders, notwithstanding the badness of the weather, and their earnest entreaties, could obtain no quarter. On some of them going into an inn to prepare some food for the children, who were perishing with cold and hunger, the fire was extinguished, and they were, with threatenings of the lash, driven out of the town. Several were refused the necessaries for the journey, though they offered to purchase them with money. More than once, the weary were directed to sheds and hog-sties, when there was no want of better accommodation; and sometimes they were even obliged to encamp, amid storm and rain, in the open air. It is true that such treatment was contrary to the will of the supreme authorities, nor was it repeated to those who came after.

In the Bohemian towns of Teutschbrod, Czaslau, Königingrätz, and Trautenau, they experienced no unpleasantness of any kind.

CHAPTER VI.

Arrival and settlement of the Zillerdalers in Silesia—Entry into
Michelsdorf—Day of rest there—Arrival in Schmiedeberg—
Thanksgiving-day—Distribution of Bibles—Schools for the
old and young among the Zillerdalers—Their reception into
the national compact, and into the established Protestant
church—They partake of the Holy Eucharist under both
kinds—Provisional committee for the strangers—Bible instruction—The Zillerdalers celebrate the anniversary of the
Reformation in Fischbach—They are visited by a Silesian
at Schmiedeberg—Joy and sorrow in the congregation—
Testimonials concerning the Emigrants—Concluding re-
flections.

AT the mountain village of Michelsdorf, in the
circle of Landshut, the exiles first trod their new
fatherland.   They received their first welcome
on the 20th of September, 1837, from the Protestant pastor Bellman, who was followed by the
greater part of his flock.   The train consisted of
about a hundred and twenty persons.   At its head
advanced the fathers and mothers, tall and well-
proportioned figures, wearing the well-known Ty-

H

rolese hat, and carrying umbrellas; otherwise habited in the simple costume of their country. Among all, it was easy to perceive that their dress had been newly provided for the journey. Earnest and still the procession moved forward; even the spectators, penetrated with sympathy, observed a deep silence: firm, tranquil resolution was expressed in the countenances of the men, humble resignation in those of the women. These were followed by ten or twelve wagons carrying the aged and sick, women and children, as well as the most necessary articles of their moveable property. Then there came several small two-wheeled cars, drawn by their owners, containing their books, &c.

About noon, on the twenty-third of September, the second train arrived, consisting of two hundred and eighteen persons, among whom was John Fleidl. They had traversed, in twenty-three days, about ninety German miles. As during the last few days there had been an incessant rain, the travellers here halted some hours, in order to recruit themselves for the mountain pass, and the remaining six miles of their journey. The countenances of all indicated the greatest exhaustion, only the children were cheerful and joyous. Pastor Bellman stepped into the midst of the

pilgrims, who, young and old, crowded round him
with tears in their eyes, endeavouring to reach his
hand and catch a glimpse of his countenance.
Every eye was fixed upon him, glistening with
emotions of joy and gratitude. One party that
was encamped near the church having procured it
to be opened, some of them entered: in silence
they ranged themselves before the altar, when pre-
sently one of them perceived, and drew the attention of his companions to, a portrait of the king:
with a general shout of the highest transport, they
all rushed towards the picture, contemplating it
with eyes beaming with tears of joy. It was, indeed, the likeness of one who, by his royal favour,
had caused their gladness at that happy moment.

On the evening of Saturday, the 30th of September, the third division arrived, with six wagons and
sixty-five persons. As the following day was to
be the harvest festival, they were invited here to
partake its rest. The overseers of the parish
anxiously provided for their accommodation, and
several of the Catholic householders also offered
them a ready welcome. On the Sunday morning,
they all appeared in the church, whither they were
conducted by the clergy; they likewise attended

the afternoon service, and all the other holy exercises. At two o'clock the next morning, they passed through Hermsdorf, where the Protestant inhabitants prepared for them breakfast, on their way to Schmiedeberg.

A few days later, a fourth division followed, consisting of three families and other individuals, about thirty in number, who had not before been able to dispose of their farms and cattle, the whole followed by a throng of foot-passengers. Pastor Bellman relates that in his conversations with the travellers, " they expressed their thankfulness to God, that, with the exception of some trifling ailments, they had all enjoyed perfect health; and that, notwithstanding the great number of those who were aged and infirm, they had not, contrary to the predictions of some of their friends, lost a single individual on the journey. There were among them many families of whose members not one remained behind; yet not a few in which parents from children, children from parents, and brothers and sisters, had been parted. Their separation must, indeed, have been in the highest degree painful, and gladly would they have remained in their beloved fatherland, had not their ardent desire to be able to serve the Lord, in the liberty of their own convictions, overborne all other considerations."

The town of Schmiedeberg was appointed to the assembled emigrants as their first place of abode. As the first division arrived earlier than was expected, and as it was the season of the yearly fair, they were provided with a temporary home in Upper Schmiedeberg. Here they, as well as their followers, met with the kindest reception from the inhabitants. On Sunday, the 24th of September, those who had first arrived attended divine service in the Protestant Church. Pastor Süssenbach offered on their behalf an earnest prayer; Pastor Neumann in his sermon admonished the congregation to receive the Tyrolese with love as their Christian brethren, remarking on the powerful faith by which they must have been actuated to forsake house and home, their native country, friends and kindred, and all that man in this life holds most dear, in order to attain liberty of conscience and belief.

On the 8th of October they all came to the church, to observe a day of public thanksgiving for their happy arrival. The Zillerdalers assembled in the great open *Place* before the church, at the

doors of which the clergy stood to receive them.
The hymn was sung—

> " When Christ his Church defends,
>   All hell may rage and riot,
>   Nor mortal foes nor fiends
>   Shall give her long disquiet;
>   He who at God's right hand doth sit
>   Shall quell all foes beneath her feet," &c.

The church-doors were now thrown open, and
the clergy led in the people, singing the hymn—

> " Up, Christians, ye who in Him trust,
>   And let no threats affrighten."

To the Exiles were allotted the seats on the
right and left before the altar. Divine service
commenced with the hymn—

> " In Thee, O God, I put my trust."

Then followed an address from the altar; and the
whole was concluded by singing,

> " Now thank God, one and all," &c.

The church could hardly contain the crowds
that streamed in from all directions; while all
manifested the most hearfelt interest and sympathy.

In the same week, all the heads of families, as
well as the unmarried, were summoned to the

town-hall, where they were presented with Bibles, by Pastor Siegert. With tears of joy and gratitude, they received the gift. Among these was one man, the father of a family, who, though only forty years old, had long been gray from grief and anxiety, and had left his wife and children in the valley, as they still adhered to the Romish Church.

The government at once made provision for the instruction both of the children and the adults. A schoolmaster from the Royal Seminary at Buntzlau was appointed for this purpose. Daily, from the hours of eight till twelve, above eighty Tyrolese children, between the ages of six and fifteen, are instructed in the school. From two till five, ninety adults are taught reading, writing, arithmetic, singing, and Bible history. From four o'clock till five, about twenty aged persons are taught the art of reading. "Cost what it may," they said, "we must learn to read the Bible."

On the 13th of October, being the birthday of their noble benefactress the Princess Marianne of Prussia, the school was consecrated, and the schoolmaster inducted; after which, the president of the province, Dr. Von Merckel, addressed first the children, and then the adults, saluting them all as the new subjects of the King.

Unfortunately, the schools could not be opened till towards the end of the month, as the Asiatic cholera had broken out in the town, which also carried off some of the new inhabitants. The clergy were constant in their attendance on the sufferers, many visiting them two or three times daily. In consequence of their intercourse on these and other occasions, both in private and in the sanctuary, there soon arose a closer intimacy between the clergy and the Tyrolese. By these means, the former became so well satisfied of the people's soundness and steadiness in the principles of the Protestant faith, that on the 12th of November they were, in the presence of Prince William and his consort, admitted into the national church. After Fleidl had, in behalf of all, read their confession of faith, the others standing around the altar, they, for the first time, partook of the eucharist under both kinds, Prince William preceding the men, and the Princess the women, to that holy sacrament. A number of young people were also admitted, who had been previously prepared by the clergy.

Many instances might now be noted of the kindness shewn to them by the inhabitants of Schmiedeberg. A merchant undertook to count and sort all their money, previous to its being deposited in the royal bank at Breslau. Several matrons instructed the young females in domestic employments, &c.

The neighbourhood also around Schmiedeberg manifested no want of sympathy to the Zillerdalers. Under the auspices of the Dowager Countess von Reden, at Buchwald, a provisional committee was formed on their behalf. The Countess herself superintended their interests with especial zeal, and shewed to them the kindness of a mother; indeed, by this name they were accustomed to designate that pious lady.

The Tyrolese frequently attended a weekly lecture by Pastor Haupt of this place, who expounded, with especial reference to them, the Epistle to the Romans: also other neighbouring clergy held with them hours of public devotion.

Pastor Siegert of Fischbach having been charged with the spiritual necessities of the new-comers, proceeded at once with all due fidelity to his task, holding meetings with the adults in the evenings, three times a week, at which not only the emigrants, but also many of the inhabitants, resorted with regular attendance. Here the fundamental doctrines of Christianity, with their mutual con-

nexion and dependence, as well as the principal
Protestant Confessions, were clearly and familiarly
exhibited without any admixture of polemics.

The attention, sympathy, and desire for instruction manifested by all were in the highest degree
encouraging. On the 29th of October, the customary festival to commemorate the Reformation
was held in the church at Fischbach, to which
the Zillerdalers came over from Schmiedeberg.
Here they found a numerous congregation : among
those present was the family of Prince William,
brother of the King. On this occasion, Pastor
Siegert selected for his lecture that part of the
history of the Reformation which especially related
to the Saltzburg Exiles.

Four men of known experience and understanding were chosen from their number to preside over
the little community. These were Heim, Brucker,
Stock, and Fleidl, who watched over the general
welfare, and superintended the others' occupations,
which consisted chiefly in the felling of timber.
Although they were not so capable as the natives
of employments requiring so much exertion, they
yet, on the other hand, shewed great fondness
and endurance of continuous labour.

The strangers also received several visits from

their neighbours in Hirschberg. One of these thus expresses himself, under date September 30:—

"I have just returned from a visit to the Protestants of Zillerthal, and ardently wish that I could transfer to my paper somewhat of that warmth and freshness of impression which I derived from the reality, and which I cannot otherwise describe than as at once exciting both the deepest melancholy and the liveliest joy. Melancholy must the sight ever be of uncorrupt human nature violently torn from its maternal soil, where, with all life's fibres, it had been long deeply rooted, and suddenly transplanted into a foreign region. And though I scarcely think that these plain, unsophisticated men, so far removed from all sickly sentimentality, were conscious of this feeling, yet was it, as by a kind of instinct, sufficiently indicated in the somewhat dejected, almost anxious appearance of their otherwise energetic, trust-inspiring countenances. Nevertheless, the aspect of these simple natures was most cheering and refreshing to the heart, as clearly manifesting that in them there dwelt no fraud or guile. The occasion of my visit was the announcement of a religious festival as about to take place in the church at Schmiedeberg, on account of the Protestant Zillerdalers. Several inhabitants of the neighbouring Hirschberg also took the same journey, among whom was the superintendent of the diocese. Immediately, however, on our first entering Schmiedeberg, we perceived that it could not be a church festival that was approaching, as the good Zillerdalers were going about in anything but their Sunday dress. At the same time, we observed that it was not with the picturesque, somewhat theatrically costumed Tyrolese, whom one is accustomed to see travelling about the country, that we now had to do; rather we were reminded, by their coarse brown smockfrocks and broad-brimmed black hats, of the Sclavonian pot-menders.* On the other hand, the powerful, broad-shouldered figures of the men, as well as their honest, pious features, spoke much in their favour. At the very outset of our intercourse with them, we recognised the true-hearted, open character, the honest, simple mind, the childlike, confiding spirit of uncorrupt human nature. They related to us their endurances on the journey, how

---

* Literally, pot-binders. (*Topfbinder.*) These are itinerant mechanics from Sclavonia, who are remarkable for their unequalled skill and dexterity in binding hoops of wire around the earthen pots which are extensively used in Bohemia for culinary and other purposes, and which, of course, but for such precaution, would be very liable to be speedily broken.

many hád been obliged to spend the night without shelter, how on several occasions they had been pointed at with the finger of scorn, and sometimes assailed with stones. Often the places where they sat, as if thereby they had been polluted, were washed before their eyes. However incredible such a thing may sound, yet so far were their honest minds from all fanciful exaggerations, that one cannot refuse credit to the statement. In all their declarations, they displayed a straightforward, sound understanding, a pious trust in God, without any taint of cant or hypocrisy. That they were familiar with the Holy Scriptures has already sufficiently been made known; and it was ever near their hearts to possess a Bible of their own. On this occasion we inquired for the dwelling of John Fleidl, and some of those present immediately offered to conduct us to it. And here I cannot omit relating a little incident which may appear not devoid of interest. On the way, a beggar met us, and whilst I stood a moment talking with him, my Zillerdalian guide observed at a short distance a pair of horse-shoes, but little the worse for wear, lying upon the ground. Scarcely had the beggar perceived this, than he took them out of his hand, and wished to keep them for himself. The Ziller-

daler gave them to him, but remarked at the same
time that they could not belong to him, and might
be the property of one of his countrymen, whose
horse was standing in the neighbourhood; whereupon I took them from the beggar, and delivered
them again to the finder. As we stayed a long
time with Fleidl, my conductor in the meanwhile
had gone away; by-and-bye he came up to me,
saying, 'Now they are in the right place.' He
had in the meantime been busying himself in
finding out from what horse the shoes had fallen,
and causing them to be replaced. I could mention
many other striking instances of their strict con-
scientiousness, and regard to the rights of property,
which were related to us during our visit. The
appearance of Fleidl is just as simple and unas-
suming as that of his countrymen. He is tall and
powerful, as are most of the Zillerdalers. We
found him in his coarse linen shirt-sleeves, busied
with the affairs of his community, and surrounded
by several venerable old men, true *sancti patres* of
the poet; and altogether the scene forcibly reminded one of ' the Judge' in Göthe's Herrmann
and Dorothea. Fleidl enjoys great respect among
his companions, which is entirely due to his in-
tegrity, as he is one of the poorer class. All besides

that we heard in Schmiedeberg concerning the Zillerdalers spoke loudly in their favour.

" A merchant there, who had entertained about forty in his spacious mansion, could not sufficiently extol their unaffected piety, probity, and trustworthiness. One of these was the man who had separated from his wife and eight children, as they would not accompany him, which circumstance caused him inconsolable grief throughout his journey.

" Nine members of the congregation reached the land which they had so earnestly desired only to be soon called away to their everlasting home. Five were snatched away, after a few hours of painful suffering, by the above-mentioned malady. They died with tranquil resignation and believing confidence, not without lively, heartfelt gratitude that they had attained that which they had so ardently longed for—the enjoyment of the holy Eucharist, and the certainty of finding a resting-place for their inanimate dust in a Protestant churchyard. Many, indeed, had emigrated solely that they might enjoy this blessing. Ignatius Hauser, a man aged sixty-six, and who had been three years crippled with paralysis, came with his will in his pocket; and a matron, who had passed her eightieth year, had on the journey continually urged her children to make haste lest she should die before they reached the new fatherland. The desires of both were fulfilled; a few days after their arrival, they joyfully raised their languishing heads with the thanksgiving, 'Lord, now lettest thou thy servant depart in peace.' The congregation was also increased by the birth of two children, one of whom was a daughter, that, an hour after the arrival of the first train, beheld at once the light of the world and its parents' new home, and under favourable circumstances, since, as soon as they heard of the event, the noble family of Schulenberg afforded the mother an immediate shelter in their hospitable mansion. The noble host himself stood sponsor to the child, which received the name of Frederica Wilhelmina. Several marriages also speedily followed. The account of these events was furnished by the oft-named John Fleidl."

Let us now hear the testimony of an approved witness concerning the present condition of the Zillerdalers in Schmiedeberg.*

---

* It must be borne in mind that Dr. Rheinwald's narrative was written before the Zillerdalers were located in Erdmannsdorf, their destined home, while they were still sojourning in Schmiedeberg.

"Earnestly desirous for the pure Word of God, they embraced with visible joy every opportunity of hearing its announcements, and are filled with gratitude for the happy turn which their affairs have taken, through the gracious mediation of our king. At the same time, they do not conceal the sorrow and pain they felt on parting from those whom they left in the valley: 'However,' they said, 'we parted from one another in peace.' And they rejoice over the victory which they then achieved, and only lament for those who, against their inward convictions, still held back. They speak without bitterness concerning the oppressions which they have endured, regarding them rather as the means necessary for the trial and purification of their faith. 'It must needs all have so happened,' they said, 'in order to attain such a glorious end.' Very many of them possess a comprehensive, fundamental acquaintance with Scripture, which they know well how to employ most effectually towards every one who asks a reason for their belief; and all maintain sound religious principles, without any partialities, eccentricities, or exaggerations. They are indeed healthy children of the vigorous times of the Reformation.

" Besides the writings which have been already mentioned as having conduced to their awakening and confirmation, I found in the possession of one man ' Stolz's New Testament,' and his ' Annotations,' for which he had paid a high price in Zillerthal. I counselled him to lay aside this apparatus until he should find that he did not need it. Unhappily, there had been no want of endeavours on the part of some to impress them with a special religious type, which, however, their sound understandings enabled them immediately to detect; nor indeed was it, in general, so easy to entangle those whose bias under ecclesiastical oppression had necessarily been in a Protestant direction, and who had long struggled after liberty, in another yoke of bondage.

" Others, again, have not failed to question whether the Zillerdalers, so simple-minded and conversant with the plain Word of God, could cordially unite with a good conscience to our national church, as they had been pre-occupied with Luther's writings and the Augsburg Confession. Not long ago, some Zillerdalers resorted with their horses, whose keep had become too burdensome, to a market at some distance, in order to sell them. Their way thither lay through a

town, where their appearance excited great observation; and some of the inhabitants, being desirous of imparting their own religious peculiarities,
shewed them great kindness, and invited them to
share their repast. 'We consented,' (so one of
them related it with inimitable *naiveté*,) 'for we
could not well refuse the offer of a meal'; but we
soon perceived, from their impetuous, quarrelsome
discourse, that there was a sect here; whereupon
we kept silence, thanked them, and went on our
way.' Such incidents most plainly intimate of
what Spirit they were the offspring. To the
fathers of families, especially, it was matter of the
greatest satisfaction that they could now send
their children to a Protestant school. They lead
among us a quiet, orderly life, displaying unaffected, harmless good nature; an earnest, tranquil,
firm demeanour, a clear understanding, which,
even in matters to which they are unaccustomed,
speedily finds the right way. The aged Heim
does not conceal 'that there are some' wayward
sheep in the flock:' but of a marked character
these are very few. They are very desirous of
exchanging their present temporary condition for
their place of final settlement. 'We are,' they
say, 'not accustomed to eat our bread without

working for it.' In short, we are firmly persuaded that when they shall have been placed in circumstances corresponding, as far as possible, to their former rural way of life, it will be more and more manifest that Prussia has no reason to repent of having received them into its mountains and valleys."

The fulfilment of this wish is on the point of being realized. According to certain intelligence, they are to remain very near the place of their present sojourn.

Quite in harmony with the testimony just cited are other reports communicated from Silesia.

" They avail themselves with zeal and fidelity, not only of the schools, but also of the public week and Sunday services, as well as the hours of evening instruction; and make a just and pious use of the Holy Scriptures, of which abundant copies are diffused among them. Hitherto, nothing has occurred to shake the good opinion with which the best members of the Protestant Church were first induced to regard their new brethren."

And another, " It is very gratifying that the polemical aspect which the emigrants were naturally obliged to assume towards the Romish Church has produced no disturbance. They unite, with all the freshness of their Protestant feeling, a bene-volent mildness and placability towards that which so bitterly, opposed them, and occasioned them so much calamity. They are also free from all kinds of sectarianism. I believe that these (in the best sense) virtuous, open, and simple natures would of themselves spurn away all attempts to lead them into such devious paths, which yet have not been wanting."

On the other hand, it is asserted in some reports issued from the city of Brixen, where, on account of its proximity to the scene, the facts might be truly ascertained: " Religion is with many, pro-bably the greater number of the Zillerdalers, only a secondary consideration. The prospect of a good reception in Prussia, the probable predilection of the king, the desire for intrigues and unre-strained marriages, an inclination for greater liberty, which is especially dear to the Zillerdaler, particu-larly the imaginary honour of firmly maintaining an opinion once expressed, the presumed disgrace, and therefore false shame, of retracting and failing in one's profession; these are the motives which commonly induce persons to change their religion."

To the honour of the Catholic Church, how-ever, it must be observed, that not all its organs of

opinion took this perverse and prejudiced view of
the affairs of the Zillerdalers. We find in some,
other principles guiding their judgment on this
matter. Thus, a journal,* edited by a body of
Catholic clergy and laymen, requires of certain inhabitants of Hermestan, who were going to Rome,
" that they should call at Zillerthal, in order to
ascertain with their own eyes whether their apo-
logy for the measures of the Austrian government
against these poor dwellers upon the mountains,
who now are no longer Roman Catholics, but desire a little church of their own, were just or not;
and whether the Toleration-Edicts of Joseph were
not more suitable to our times than the limitation
of the same suggested by the Crypt of Jesuits."

Thus far the narrative by Dr. Rheinwald: it is
only necessary to add the information of a high
authority, derived from unquestionable sources,
that " during the winter they were taken care of
in Schmiedeberg, and in summer they entered
upon their new possessions in the domains of
Erdmannsdorf, where each obtained a house and
farm suitable to his means and his former position
in the Tyrol. The colony itself has received the

* "Allgemeine Kirchenzeitung für Deutschland und Schweitz,
Mai, 1837."

name of their old home, Zillerthal. Reports have, we know, been circulated, that the exiles are discontented, and already wish to emigrate again; but nothing could be more untrue. Those of the labouring class who are accustomed to leave the Tyrol annually in search of employment continue their periodic migrations, and are readily furnished by the Prussian government with passports for the purpose. The great majority, whom no such necessity compels, remain stationary;—all are happy, and thankful for the kindness with which they have been received, and the liberty of conscience which they enjoy.

"Such is the simple narrative of this Austrian oppression, and of the happy deliverance of its victims. Prudence forbade the fires and massacres, the dragonades and confiscations of former centuries; but the denial of justice, the withholding of the religious liberty guaranteed by the law, the refusal of Christian burial, and the most barbarous and unnatural prohibition to enter into the marriage state, concluded at last by an expulsion from house and home, can be designated by no milder term than that of persecution. When Protestants speak of the flames of Smithfield, or the horrors of St. Bartholomew's night, they are told that these

things are not to be imputed to the religion of
Rome, but to the barbarism of the age. They
then point to the unprincipled perfidy which suggested, and the wanton cruelty which accompanied,
the revocation of the Edict of Nantes; but again
the times are made to bear the blame. The Saltzburg persecution, conducted by a Romish archbishop, rises up in the Protestant mind as proof
that in the eighteenth century the practice of
Popery was still the same; but it is once more
replied, that the true principles of civilization and
toleration were not understood till within the last
forty years. The history of the Zillerdale Exiles
comes to testify that even in the present age of
supposed illumination the system of Rome remains
unchanged—as intolerant, as tyrannical, as faith-
less, as it was in the darkest of the ages that have
passed away.

" Who that knows anything of the kind and
amiable dispositions of the late or the present Emperor of Austria would believe that any power on
earth could have transformed them into the relent-
less oppressors of their loyal subjects, or induced
them to break a distinct promise, and deliberately
to violate the express articles of the most solemn
treaties? It is beyond all doubt that no temporal

power could have moved them to measures so re-
pugnant to their nature and their honour; but
Popery has blinded them to the perception of right
and wrong, and made them insensible even to
shame. There can be neither doubt nor mistake
about the matter. The Treaty of Westphalia, the
Toleration-Edicts of Joseph II., and the Act of the
Germanic Confederation, bound the Emperors of
Austria to secure liberty of conscience to their
subjects; and by the persecution of the Zillerdalers
these solemn international engagements have all
been violated; a fact not very creditable to the
house of Hapsburg, but momentously instructive
to Protestant nations and churches. They may
learn that all Popish professions of liberality, or
concern for liberty of conscience, are hypocritical;
that if there be such a thing as religious liberty
in the world, it is because God in his goodness has
turned the scale of power and might in favour of
Protestantism; and that if ever by our folly, or as
a punishment for our sins, the Papists should become the strongest, that moment Europe will cease
to breathe the free air of Christian freedom.
Wherever Popery now possesses the power, liberty
of conscience is unknown. The Pope suffers it
not in his own dominions. He has of late com-

pelled the benevolent King of Sardinia to abrogate almost all the old privileges of the Waldenses. Bavaria returns to intolerance, and compels her Protestant soldiers to pay homage to the wafer. Austria contracts the little measure of freedom which her statutes had provided, and forcibly drives Protestantism out of the Tyrol. Popery is still the same in her dispositions, her aim, and her means, and therefore Protestant nations must still entertain the same distrust, and exercise the same vigilance, that they did two centuries ago. There can be no peace with Rome—nor any security for liberty of conscience—except in the continued existence of European Protestant ascendancy. It is a sad fact, of which this history reminds us, namely, that neither sovereigns nor churchmen of the Roman school can be bound by treaties or oaths; that fear is the only motive, and force the only argument, that can induce them to maintain a semblance of mercy and veracity. Thankful we may be that, by the fundamental law of the land, this system of cruelty and fraud is for ever excluded from the British throne."— *Quar. Rev.* vol. lxiv. pp. 139—141.

APPENDIX:

CONTAINING

EXTRACTS FROM SOME ORIGINAL LETTERS

BY THE ZILLERDALERS.

1831.—" WE are astonished that the ' People's Friend' has so belied us; because we well know that not one among us has gone back. Instead of becoming fewer, our number has greatly increased. Now we see how they wish to overwhelm our simple minds with falsehoods of which we know nothing. But the Most High, who sees, as with a glance, through all the designs of men, yea, His providence, most beloved friend, has so ordered it, that you should set forth the truth for us; God be thanked, and you also; we fully recognise the kindness which you have manifested on our behalf. We all rejoiced when we received your assurance of all possible help—thanks be to you through Jesus Christ. We also hope that God will graciously grant to our cause a happy issue, that so we may be able to hear the sound doctrine of the Gospel, and be freed from those who only multiply darkness, who use the Word of God as a cloak

124 APPENDIX.

for their own sinful, empty prattle; who, as Christ says, 'Make void the Word of God by their traditions.' What communion has the living with the dead? We adore the Triune God whom they know not; for it is written, 'I will not give my glory unto another.' (Isaiah, xlviii. 11.) If, now, most beloved friend, the idol-priests, who think gain to be godliness, tell you anything, believe it not. They pervert the Word of God in their mouths, and speak vanities and lies, meditating untruth in their hearts. With their lips they shew kindness to a man, while they secretly lie in wait for him. Therefore we again pray you for your support. Who appointed the ravens to bring Elijah food, but the all-providing God? Even He who led your hearts with such kindness towards us. Our number is now two hundred and thirty-six. When I informed the government that my grandfather had died, I was commanded to bury him in the open field. It is well, I said, that place and station cause neither our blessedness nor condemnation.

"F."

1832.—"We pray you from the bottom of our hearts to grant us your assistance, for indeed we know not how to help ourselves. Our number is about a hundred and fifty. There are besides many others who would join us, but they first wish to see how the affair will terminate, for they are of opinion it will not go well with us. Meanwhile, we stand fast by the Holy Scriptures, and the unaltered Augsburg Confession, as it was accepted by the Emperor Charles V. in the year, 1530. God be praised for granting us such light! We have a sure word of prophecy, from which the apostle says to those who deviate, ' It were better for them not to have known the way of righteousness, than, after they have known it, to turn from the holy commandment delivered unto them :' (2 Peter ii. 21 ;) and St. Paul· exhorts Timothy, ' But continue thou in the things which thou hast learned and hast been assured of, knowing of whom thou hast learned them,' &c. (2 Tim. iii. 14, 15.) Beloved friends, I must say yet one thing more, that several of us have not for many years received the sacrament from the Romish party ; I myself have not for four years, because they administer it under only one form, contrary to the commandment of Christ our Lord. I cannot describe the dreadful insults which we have endured from the priesthood. May God forgive them !

" H."

1834.—" The Emperor has promised us equal rights with the Catholics ; and when we prayed him to grant us a dismissal, he replied, ' It is indeed against my inclination, nevertheless, I will see what can be done.' He bade us thereupon still to remain constant, and not to play the hypocrite. But now they oppress us as far as they are able. The persecutions, which we have already described to you, still continue, and indeed become more and more severe. Wherever a Protestant is found among Catholics, he is compelled to depart, or if he desires to purchase any property, the entire parish is summoned to prevent him. They also take away our books ; and if any one falls sick, he is forbidden any visits, save those of the priests, who hasten to condemn him on his sick-bed, and predict his eternal damnation. The passport which we requested to go to the Emperor has been refused.

" F. and H."

"We pray to God and you for help, and hope He will be pleased to send us a deliverer, even as He sent Moses to the Israelites, to free us from our oppressors. Pharaoh the king carried it with a high hand until he found his grave in the Red Sea. Even so can God deliver us. Therefore we beseech you to do for us all things possible, and not to forget us, as we also will not forget you."

———————

1835.—"We thank God on every remembrance of the kindness and compassion which you bear towards us ; for the books you sent us, and for all things else. They still oppress us as far as possible, only they have not put any to death ; but nothing besides has been omitted.

"F., R., and H."

———————

1837.—Addressed to a Protestant Clergyman.

"Most beloved friend and brother in Christ Jesus—

"As you desire us to report to you how it fared with us upon our journey, we are not willing any longer to delay. We beg you not to take it ill on our part that we sent you no account before. The reason was, that we wished to wait till all had arrived, that we might communicate the latest information. We felt very anxious on account of some, who, we were told at Böcklabruck, were only sixteen miles behind us ; but after waiting for them several days in Schmiedeberg, and not being able to obtain any certain tidings of them, we resolved, on the 29th of September, to take out a passport to go and meet them. But, God be thanked, we had not proceeded further than the borders at Konigshain, when we met them safe and sound, and with a joyful welcome. As to what else befel us, we need only say, that we everywhere met with a kind reception. Everywhere we found good quarters; no one laid any obstacles in our way. Some of the first division were obliged indeed to encamp under the open heaven. But, thanks to God, it was not so with us; for the hand of the Lord guided us all the way, until we came into our new fatherland. Those who arrived last, spake in like manner.

. " Thus have the words been fulfilled which we heard to our comfort in a sermon at Efferding, ' Have ye ever lacked anything ?' and with the disciples we must answer, ' Nothing.' We wish also to inform you, that five of our number already lie buried in Schmiedeberg. Three of them were carried off by the cholera, the other two of bodily weakness; one of the first was a youth of twelve years, the rest of an advanced age. Now, Holy Father! thy will be done, which always and at all times is the best. Thus, no sooner had they accomplished this earthly journey, than they were called away to their heavenly home; yet not before they had partaken the most holy Supper of the Lord, for which they had so earnestly longed; after which they left the world in peace, calmly resigned to the will of God.

" At present we are unable to say more, as we have not yet received his Majesty's decision as to our final abode. We all receive from our gracious Lord the King, each his wages in due proportion. And now, most beloved brothers in Christ, we greet you all, and heartily thank you for all that you have done for us on our journey. We must confess, indeed, that we were not worthy of the kindness and compassion which you have shewn to us.

" May our gracious God reward you, both in time and eternity!

" *Schmiedeberg,* 14*th of October,* 1837."

THE END.

T. C. Savill, Printer, 107, St. Martin's Lane.

CPSIA information can be obtained
at www.ICGtesting.com
Printed in the USA
BVHW090828220219
540922BV00020B/1179/P

9 781331 505044